A Primer for the Inner-City School is a curriculum for the primary grades, based upon recent research in the areas of cognitive development and behavior modification. It also deals with the administration and organization of such a school, including such matters as training of paraprofessionals and working with parent groups.

This book differs significantly from recent publications dealing with the education of the inner-city child, presenting concrete, detailed suggestions for teaching procedures and instructional materials to be used. Special features include chapters on the pre-school program, perception training, and curriculum innovations such as "uncommon learning centers."

A Primer for the Inner-City School will be a valuable supplementary book for both pre-service and in-service courses dealing with education for the inner-city child, early childhood education, and curriculum theory.

Dr. Greta Morine's experience in the New York State public schools includes work with bilingual first graders and the rural disadvantaged. While teaching at Hofstra University she trained undergraduate students to work in Headstart programs and after-school programs for disadvantaged children in suburban Long Island communities. She has published articles and movies on the cognitive development of young children.

The Drs. Morine are co-authors with Neil Postman of *Discovering Your Language,* Holt, Rinehart and Winston, 1963, a junior high textbook in linguistics.

Dr. Harold Morine's experience in the public schools of New York State includes several years of teaching "educationally disenfranchised" and emotionally disturbed children. While serving as chairman of the Department of Elementary Education at Hofstra University on Long Island, he trained undergraduate students to work with inner-city children in a public school in Queens, testing out several of the curriculum ideas developed in this book. He has also served as a consultant to the Education Improvement Program at Duke University, a Ford Foundation project on inner-city education.

A PRIMER FOR THE INNER-CITY SCHOOL

McGRAW-HILL BOOK COMPANY
New York   San Francisco   St. Louis
Düsseldorf   London   Mexico
Panama   Sydney   Toronto

A PRIMER FOR THE INNER-CITY SCHOOL

HAROLD MORINE
San Jose State College

GRETA MORINE
California State College, Hayward

This book was set in Linofilm Baskerville by Applied Typographic Systems and printed on permanent paper and bound by Vail-Ballou Press. The designer was Janet Bollow. The editors were Nathaniel LaMar and Stuart A. Kenter. Charles A. Goehring supervised production.

A PRIMER FOR THE INNER-CITY SCHOOL

Printed in the United States of America.
Library of Congress catalog card number: 74-115150
1234567890   VBVB   79876543210

PREFACE

The writing of this book was undertaken largely as a result of our attempts to train college students to work with disadvantaged children. In searching the literature for appropriate reading material, we found that most of the available books were devoted to *describing* the inner-city child and delineating the *problems* of teaching these children, but few offered more than token suggestions on how to deal with these problems. What seemed to be sadly lacking was a comprehensive proposal on how to educate the inner-city child. This book presents such a proposal.

It is our contention that the school as an institution must focus upon the *educational* problems of the *child* if it is to function successfully. The school curriculum is the most critical factor in the success or failure of the school as an educational institution. This book, therefore, takes the form of a curriculum proposal, focusing on the goals, the instructional materials, and the teaching procedures most appropriate and effective for inner-city children.

In developing the proposal, we have drawn from the research in behavior modification, cognitive development, and discovery methodology. Some may find this a strange combination of sources, but we hope that a careful study of the proposal will convince the reader that they are in fact logically compatible. We have dealt with the early school years (preschool through the second grade) because these are the most crucial years in determining the educational success or failure of the inner-city child.

This book can be most useful in college courses dealing with the teaching of the inner-city child, early childhood programs, and curriculum theory or construction. We hope it will also be of value to administrators and teachers working on the "firing line."

We wish to thank the following people for their help: Dr. Seymour Gang, of the New York City Public Schools, for the opportunity to observe an effective program in action; Mrs. Florence Korn and Miss Evelyn Abrahams, of the Roosevelt Public Schools (Long Island), and Mr. Herman Bogden, of the New York City Public Schools, for the opportunity to take college students into the schools and try out a number of curricular ideas; Dr. Robert Spaulding, director of the Education Improvement Program at Duke University, for the opportunity to observe the successful implementation of behavior-modification techniques in combination with discovery techniques and for his comments upon the preliminary manuscript of this book; Dr. Hobert Burns, of San Jose State College, Dr. Bruce Joyce, of Teachers College, Columbia, Dr. Tudor Jones, of California State College at Hayward, and Charles Swensen, of Hofstra University, for reading and commenting upon portions of the preliminary manuscript; Dr. Caleb Gattegno, of Educational Solutions, Inc., for permission to comment upon the Cuisenaire rods and Words in Color.

HAROLD MORINE
GRETA G. MORINE

CONTENTS

A PRIMER FOR THE INNER-CITY SCHOOL

ONE: ANALYZING WHERE YOU'RE GOING

Inner-city schools are much in the news of late. It is generally agreed that these schools have failed. Many reasons are offered for their failure. Among these are the following: the teachers are prejudiced, the children are stupid, the teachers are middle class, the children are lower class, the teachers are underpaid, the children are emotionally disturbed, the "good" teachers go elsewhere, the children suffer from anomie, there aren't enough teachers, the classes are overcrowded, the parents don't care, the children lack respect for learning, the teachers are inadequately trained, there aren't enough teaching materials, the buildings are antiquated, the curriculum is middle class, there is not enough money, the schools are segregated, there is too much politics in school administration, there is not enough local control of schools, a combination of the above, all of the above.

Given so many alleged causes of the inner-city schools' failure, it is easy to propose solutions as follows: take local politics out of the schools, put more local politics in the schools, integrate the schools, segregate the schools, educate the parents, reeducate the teachers, fire the prejudiced teachers, hire larger numbers of teachers, build new schools, bus the children elsewhere, restrict the curriculum to the three R's, add more courses such as Negro history to the curriculum, spend more money, economize, do some of these, do all of these, do none of these.

We should like to suggest that there is probably some truth in each of the suggested causes of the schools' failures; but having said that, we should like immediately to note that each of these truths is overstated, oversimplified, and misleading. Further, each of the suggested solutions probably has some value and would accomplish some good from someone's point of view. These solutions fail, however, simply because they respond to causes that are overstated, oversimplified, and misleading.

In real life, there is no simple solution to a complex problem. However, in dealing with complex problems, we generally attempt to focus on only a few aspects of the problem for purposes of analysis. This is a legitimate procedure as long as one does not lose sight of the fact that the complexity still exists, and as long as the aspects focused upon are productive of possible solutions.

Given the complexity of the problem, how then is one to arrive at some notion of what an inner-city school must do and how it ought to do it? These are the two essential questions to which this book will try to respond. We shall not overly concern ourselves with why the schools are currently bad schools. Our concern is with how we can produce a school (public, private, or bootlegged) that will do the job of educating children so that they can enjoy being children and succeed as adults. To do this, we need to consider those ideas in the social sciences that will suggest the conditions necessary for success in school. We need to define what it is we wish to have children accomplish in school in order that they might succeed as adults. We need, then, to set out a plan that, when acted upon, will enable children to do the job. We need, in short, to focus our attention on what *children* will be doing in school, not what politicians, civil rights workers, teachers, administrators, parents, and editorial writers are doing.

Much of the analysis of the problem of the "disadvantaged" has focused on parents and teachers.[1] Studies have been made of their differing attitudes, values, methods of discipline, use of language, etc. The point seems to be that these differences in behavior and expectation cause conflicts in children and cannot be resolved since neither adult group is willing or able to change. This focus seems to be rather unproductive from the point of view of the educa-

[1] See, for example, the articles by Goldberg, Cloward and Jones, Wilson, and Haubrich in A. H. Passow, *Education in Depressed Areas*, New York, Bureau of Publications, Teachers College, Columbia University, 1963.

tional goal. The question is not how or why these adults have failed but, rather, how do children succeed?

Let us, then, move to our first question: What ought a school to do for its children? Having answered this question, we shall in succeeding chapters propose how to go about accomplishing the task.

THE PURPOSE OF THE INNER-CITY SCHOOL

It is a basic point that schools have no excuse for existence if they do not in some way benefit both the children who attend them and the society as a whole. Some militant blacks have tended to diminish the value of public schools, labeling them "colonial institutions." They state flatly that to succeed in such an institution is to fail as a black man. The primary function of an inner-city school in today's society must be to eliminate such a dichotomy.

Success in school, for any group of children, is more than an end in itself. It is a means to the further end of success in life, which in our society implies the attainment of some measure of personal satisfaction as well as contributive membership in some social group, be it large or small. Obviously, not all public schools have been organized in such a way that success in school does lead to success in life. The inner-city school must restructure itself for this purpose, or it loses its function as a legitimate institution in our society.

Success in the American junior or senior high school and in the American college is primarily a function of two factors. The first is a desire to succeed in these institutions. The second is an ability to read and to read well. It may well be that much of what is taught and learned in these places is useless, and some of it is, perhaps, harmful. It may even be true that one must often get a "higher" education in spite of, rather than because of, the schools. It is nevertheless true that for the vast majority who attain success in our society the schools are the means or the vehicle that makes success possible. The schools are the gateway to the tens of thousands of positions that offer personal satisfaction as well as good money. If this were not the case, there would be no need to be concerned if the inner-city schools were bad.

There is no longer any question in our mind that desire will carry a child a long way in school. Desire and the ability to read will carry one even further. Clearly, without each of these it is only a question of time before the child runs into repeated failure and quits the school system. Even while still *in* the system he may have quit. He remains in the system only because society won't let him quit. Society requires that the young attend school. Society doesn't always require that the young learn while in school. When a child succeeds in the school as a scholar, he increases his chances to succeed in society. Our primary ends for the school, then, are to develop a desire for success in school and to teach the child to be an excellent reader.

These two ends, desire to succeed in school and success in reading, are intimately related to each other and to other matters. Desire, for example, is related to a child's self-concept. A child who thinks of himself as a good student wants to go to school, wants to study, wants to maintain his self-concept of being a good student. Human beings strive very hard to maintain their self-concepts. They strive particularly hard to maintain a self-concept when society in general, and people whom they respect in particular, value the ideals imbedded in the self-concept. When, then, a student has a self-concept that gives him the desire to succeed in school and he faces the task of reading, it is important that he succeed in learning to read. If he fails to read, his self-concept is altered in that he cannot reconcile this failure with his self-concept of being a good student. His self-concept will adjust to the reality of his failure, and his desire is undermined. Conversely, if he succeeds in the task of learning to read, his self-concept of being a good student is reaffirmed (reinforced if you prefer) and his desire is strengthened.

In effect, a child who begins school by failing in an important task views himself as a failure and is viewed by others as a failure. He then tends not to push himself and not to be pushed by others to succeed in the next task. If a child is to desire success in school and to attain success in school, he must begin school by succeeding in the tasks presented to him. This is what makes kindergarten and the primary grades the crucial grades — the grades, so to speak, in which the die is cast.

The major task that faces the child in the primary grades is that of learning how to read. It is a task at which he must succeed if our two primary goals for the school are to be achieved. It follows, then, that the inner-city school must help the child to be successful in his initial reading experiences.

Now learning to read is not as difficult a task as a lot of reading experts maintain. It is, however, not an easy task. The child may fail to learn to read through no fault of his own. He may fail to learn to read because he doesn't have the visual equipment to discriminate shapes and the order of shapes in the same way you and I discriminate them. We shall come back to this topic in greater detail later, but for now we merely wish to point out that seeing is learned behavior and that the child who sees no physical difference between "b" and "d" or who views "pot" as "top" is going to have a great deal of difficulty in learning to read, if he succeeds at all. This difficulty will affect his self-concept and his desire in a negative way. The reason for this is that the child and often the teacher have no way of knowing that what the child sees isn't what we see. Not knowing this, the child concludes he is stupid. After all, most of the other children are learning to read and he isn't. Ergo, he must be stupid because everyone knows stupid people can't read. It is a short road from here to a loss of the desire to learn.

The incidence of this kind of difficulty is high among nonreaders and poor readers. Let us also note that "the failure to see," as we have called it, is not a function of social class, economic background, race, or even native intelligence. We recently tutored a fifth-grade, middle-class white girl with an IQ of 120 who had no signs of emotional difficulty, who consistently made the two mistakes noted above as well as many others. Before tutoring she tested out as a nonreader and was labeled dyslexic by three psychologists. With five months of visual training and fourteen reading lessons, she tested out with a fifth-

4

grade reading level. This is not a problem that is unique to the inner-city school. It is a problem that exists in all schools.

There is a great deal of evidence, however, to suggest that "seeing" is related to expectation; that is, we perceive that which we expect to be there and for which we consciously look.[2] The inner-city child has not been exposed to the same kinds of experiences as the middle-class child. He has not learned to expect the same kinds of things. Therefore, he does not perceive the same things. From this point of view, perception is somewhat related to social class, and the inner-city school must take particular pains to make sure its children can "see."

The implications of the above are twofold. First, the school must provide the experiences necessary for the child to learn to "see" the distinctions he must see in order to read. Second, the child must not be exposed to the needless failure of being asked to read before he is visually able to read. This means that vision testing and vision training are critical parts of a reading program. This will be discussed in more detail in Chapter 4.

Another matter highly related to reading is language. Language is also related to the ability to use reading as a vehicle to success in the schools and, later, on the job. In the use of language there is a difference between the lower-class child and the middle-class child. There is also a similarity. The similarity is that 6-year-olds, regardless of race, class, or linguistic background, know or have learned 95 percent of the linguistic structures that they hear in their environment.[3] Now the language the middle-class child hears is not necessarily "better" than the language the lower-class child hears—although our society does place a definite value on the kind of language one uses—but the middle-class child does hear a *different* kind of language.[4] For example, he hears more adverbs used in more positions than does the lower-class child. The vocabulary in the environment of the middle-class child may run into tens of thousands of words used in a variety of ways, while the inner-city child may hear relatively few complex sentences and have a much smaller vocabulary. In addition, the middle-class child probably hears more adult conversation, while the peer group is the primary source of language experience for the inner-city child. As a general rule, then, the inner-city child is at a disadvantage as he is not as well equipped with language and consequently cannot profit from his reading as well as can the middle-class child.

The more familiarity one has with the language, the more one can profit from one's reading. To learn from reading, the student must know what the written words and linguistic structures mean when they are translated into

[2]F. Fearing, "An Examination of the Conceptions of Benjamin Whorf in the Light of Theories of Perception and Cognition," in H. Hoijer, *Language in Culture*, Chicago, University of Chicago Press, 1954, 74-76.

[3]N. Brooks, *Language and Language Learning*, New York, Harcourt, Brace and Company, 1960, p. ix.

[4]B. Bernstein, "Social Structure, Language, and Learning," in A. H. Passow, *Education of the Disadvantaged*, New York, Holt, Rinehart and Winston, 1967.

sound. Reading can be defined as moving from written symbols to sound symbols, but to profit from reading, one must know what the sound means, and to a large extent this means knowing a great deal of oral language.

The implications of this for the school are several. The school needs to put the child into an environment that enables him to expand his oral language. This means that much of the linguistic environment must be new to the child, must be beyond him. Teachers who restrict their language in order to communicate to the child at his own level deprive the child of necessary exposure to an expanded linguistic environment. Lacking this exposure, the child does not increase his skill in handling the language, and his knowledge of the language grows slowly. This leads to the child being thwarted in his attempt to profit from his reading. This, in turn, leads to a weakening of self-concept and of desire for success in school. As we pointed out earlier, this develops a vicious circle of repeated failure, which in the last analysis means a devaluation of the school experience for the child.

The failure to develop adequate language also has other consequences. Rightly or wrongly, much of success in social studies, science, mathematics, etc., is a function of linguistic abilities. Thinking about history or any other subject involves a large language component. Thought without language is difficult to conceive. It is also difficult to conceive a discipline or subject-matter area without language. All occupations have language. It is the ability to handle language that gives man his uniqueness. Success in social, political, economic, and almost all affairs of man is related to the ability to use language or to misuse it, depending on one's purpose and ethics. Language is central in man's affairs, and the consequence of this is to require that the schools give the child every opportunity to develop his language abilities to the fullest. This point cannot be overstressed. Nor can it be overstressed that one goes on learning language all of one's life. The English language is a complex and wide-ranging phenomenon. It is also an ever-changing phenomenon, and accurate communication demands that one continue to respond to the demands of a changing language.

There is a further implication here. If the study of language is a lifelong occupation, we need to do more than give children opportunities to learn more language. We need also to teach them how to study language independently so that they can continue to learn more about their language once they have left school. We need, in brief, to teach children how to think about language.

Without training in the analysis of language, most of our understanding of the language we use and hear is at the unconscious level. So also is much of our reaction to the language which surrounds us an unconscious one. As the mass media increase, more and more of our information about the world comes to us in an oral rather than in a written form. Maintaining individual thought and individual opinion in a world of mass communication is not a simple task, but it is a task that can be made easier if one is able to analyze the language used in mass communication, as well as to analyze his reactions to that language. This kind of training is, perhaps, particularly imperative for children of minority groups, since most of the mass media speak with the voice of particular vested interests who do not necessarily have the welfare of minority groups in mind.

Let us briefly summarize the goals we have set to date for the child in the early school years. The summary can start in any one of several places, as the goals have an interlocking relationship, even if they differ from each other in kind. Let us start with the goal of teaching the child to "see."

GOAL	RATIONALE
1. Develop the ability to "see."	Necessary for success in reading.
2. Teach children to read.	Necessary for success in school.
3. Help children to attain success in school.	Necessary for personal satisfaction and success in social system (life) and Necessary for positive self-concept.
4. Develop positive self-concepts.	Necessary for desire, which is a requirement for continued success in reading.
5. Expand language ability.	Necessary to profit from reading, which is necessary to success in school and positive self-concept, as well as continued success in language learning, reading, and school.
6. Teach child how to study language	Necessary for independence in learning language.

Briefly we can diagram these goals as follows:

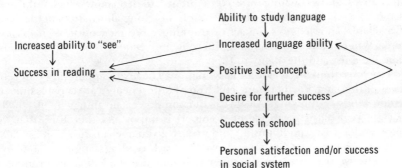

FREEDOM AND THE INNER-CITY SCHOOL

At this point it might be well to say something of the traditional goals of the school. Whatever else a school in a democracy should do, it should prepare an individual for freedom. Briefly, we hold the following as necessary conditions for freedom. To be free is to have alternatives. Implicit in the notion of alternatives is knowledge. One has no alternatives if one doesn't know what alternatives or options are available. Further, one must have knowledge of how to exercise one's options. Beyond this, one must be able to exercise the option of his choice. He must be free of restrictions. These restrictions may be legal, social, moral, psychological, or economic. In this sense of freedom, most of us are not free to buy Cadillacs because of the economic restriction. We are not free to eat caterpillars because of the psychological restriction. We are morally restricted from taking human life under most conditions. Many of us lose our opportunity to exercise certain options at income tax time because we lack knowledge as to what is an allowable deduction. Freedom, then, has many restrictions, but greater freedom can be attained through greater knowledge. Through coming to know what options are available and how to exercise these options, we can become freer. Through knowledge we gain the ability to reduce our economic, social, and psychological restrictions. Continued success in the educational system should give us much of the necessary knowledge and ability to gain increased freedom.

What we have proposed above as the goals for the primary grades is, therefore, essential to freedom. If freedom is a function of increased knowledge and abilities gained in the educational system, and if the goals we have set out for the primary grades are necessary for success in the educational system, then it follows that the goals we propose are closely related to the school's goal of preparing children to gain the benefits of a free society.

One further goal is, however, essential. In speaking of freedom, we spoke of exercising options. There is, of course, no exercising of options without a decision being made. As noted above, decisions involve knowledge, but they are more than mere knowledge. Making a decision includes being aware of alternative courses of action, identifying the probable consequences of these alternatives, and evaluating these consequences to determine which is the best or most acceptable. The act of deliberately weighing alternatives in the light of available knowledge is the act of thinking. Free men must, of necessity, think. Where there is no thinking, there is no freedom. To our list of goals, then, we must add the ability to think.

Teaching thinking is not an easy matter. There are apparently different kinds of thinking. Furthermore, children of different ages are capable only of certain kinds of thinking. An 8-year-old can do certain things intellectually that a 4-year-old is incapable of doing. It is important, therefore, that we know under what conditions a child at any given age can function intellectually. It is imperative that we endeavor to teach reading, language, and anything else we may teach in a manner that puts the child in an environment that meets those conditions and that enables him to solve the task before him with the intellectual equipment he possesses at the time.

Another problem with thinking is that it is a rather pervasive phenomenon. One thinks when one is learning reading, writing, language, arithmetic, bowling, hopscotch, or almost anything else. Thus, we have in each of these learning experiences an opportunity to teach the child to think. Indeed, to teach reading, writing, etc., and not teach thinking is not to further the cause of freedom one bit. To be able to reason and to use logic are important goals for the school.

Our goals, then, for the primary grades are:

1. To develop in children positive self-concepts and the desire for success;
2. To increase children's ability to "see," to think, and to study;
3. To teach children to function successfully in mathematics, reading, language, and logic.

These are the ingredients that make up the young scholar's role.

These are goals that could well apply to all schools, not just to the inner-city schools. We have tried to suggest why it is necessary to achieve them in the inner-city schools and some of the special problems in attaining them in that setting.

THE IMPORTANCE OF GOALS

What we are suggesting is that what is lacking in the inner-city schools and what is responsible for much of the difficulty surrounding them is a clear-cut set of goals that are consistent with the notions of human dignity and freedom, and a plan of action to attain those goals. It will profit the inner-city child little to have millions of dollars pumped into the inner-city schools if there is no clear notion of what is to be done with the millions. To state the goals in terms of better schools is useless. They must be stated in specific operational terms. To view the means as better materials, better teachers, and better administrators is also useless. The means must be stated in terms of specific acts of behavior that teachers and administrators will perform, the specific materials the children will use, and the specific ways the children will use the materials in order to attain those operationally stated goals.

Our thrust, then, is to argue that political, social, and economic solutions must relate to curriculum and teaching proposals if they are to be true solutions and not false promises. If one is clear on the means and the ends he wishes to pursue in his inner-city school, he then can ask what conditions of a political, social, and economic nature must be established to ensure their attainment. Much of what we shall propose in the following chapters can be implemented in the schools as they now exist and operate. The rest will require change.

We sincerely hope that the reader will find the logic of our arguments in this book compelling and that he will come to believe, as we believe, that every child in the inner-city has the right and ability to profit from an excellent educational institution. We believe that there will be no solution to the problems of the inner-city without each child receiving an excellent education.

The rest of this book is aimed at detailing how to ensure a profitable learning experience for each inner-city child. Chapter Two will deal with the kinds of interaction necessary between child and adult for developing positive self-concepts. The third chapter will present an overall description of the program. Chapter Four will deal with how to spot a child who cannot "see" and suggest programs for developing the ability to make visual discriminations. Chapter Five will describe the kindergarten program. Chapter Six will deal with the teaching of mathematics and logic in the first grade. Chapter Seven concerns itself with mathematical learning in the second grade. Chapter Eight will take up the topic of beginning reading. Chapter Nine will concern itself with how to teach the child to profit from his reading ability. Language development and the first-grade language curriculum will be covered in Chapter Ten, and Chapter Eleven will look at the second-grade language curriculum. The final chapter will deal with the administration of the curriculum we have proposed.

TWO: BEING POSITIVE

Each human being, as he matures, develops a self-concept. We have many expressions of this in everyday language. We speak of someone as being a winner or a loser, as being friendly or hostile, as a person who can handle pressure or who chokes up under pressure. Whatever characteristics we, as individuals, possess are, in large part, a function of our past history. Sometimes we insist that we have a particular characteristic, even when others say we do not possess that characteristic. Once in a while we actually have the characteristic, and the perceptions of our critics prove false. For the most part, however, we are what we are because others have seen us in a particular way, and we have come over a period of time to perform in the way that is expected by others.

It is our human need for attention that leads us to continue doing those things that gain us attention and that then become our characteristics. The quiet girl in class continues to be quiet because the teacher gives her credit and praise for being quiet. The misbehaving child misbehaves because he gets attention for misbehaving. More and more research is coming in to support the view that what is important to the child is attention.[1] This attention enhances or supports the self-concept, and support for one's self-concept is very important to human beings. A child who behaves badly in class often draws the sharp tongue or a hard slap from the teacher. The child may be required to stay after school or to stand in the hall. If this is the first time the child has performed badly, he may never exhibit the behavior again, not so much be-because he was punished, but because his basic self-concept is one that ordinarily doesn't allow him to perform in such a manner. If, however, the child often performs badly and has a self-concept of being a bad actor, the punishments and yellings of the teacher will serve as the attention he needs to reaffirm what he already knows — namely, he is a bad actor. Remarks by teachers, such as, "That's the kind of behavior we have come to expect from you," again reinforce the child's self-concept as a bad actor. The only way the child can maintain this self-concept is to continue to be a bad actor, and of course, each time he acts badly the teacher satisfies the basic need of the child for maintaining that self-concept. She gives him attention. In this view, teachers who talk quietly with a child to get him to see the error of his ways are as guilty as those who use other, more punitive, means. In each case, attention is given and the self-concept is reinforced.

MODIFYING CHILDREN'S BEHAVIOR

A number of researchers around the country have been doing a great deal of work in the area of behavior modification. For those interested in reading the research in detail, a list of references is included at the end of the book. From this work and from our own experience, we come to a simple principle for teachers, principals, and other adults to work from in shaping the behavior of children. Gain the child's respect and then give him attention when he is doing what you want him to do. The converse of this is to ignore the child who is doing what you do not want him to do. Put another way: the child gets attention when he is performing the role you have set out for him. The teacher's task is not to look for wrongdoers but "rightdoers." This goes against the grain of many adults who work with children. That's unfortunate, but our job is to develop healthy self-concepts in children, not to yield to our own

[1] A. Bandura and R. H. Walters, *Social Learning and Personality Development*, New York, Holt, Rinehart and Winston, 1963. See also L. P. Ullman and L. Krasner, *Case Studies in Behavior Modification*, New York, Holt, Rinehart and Winston, 1965.

psychological needs and neuroses. The research is clear in pointing out that the most irrascible of children can be brought around to performing in the "correct" manner inside of three weeks.

The problem, simply stated, is to define for the child the role he is to play and, once he begins to play that role, to interact with him in some manner. A smile will do it; a helpful comment will do it; walking over and watching him work will do it; a compliment on how well he worked when he has finished will do it; and winking works wonders. Most teachers who have difficulty with youngsters have it because they reverse this principle. The child, while he is performing his assigned tasks, is ignored. The moment he starts doing something that the teacher doesn't view as the child's role, he gets all sorts of attention. Children lose confidence in teachers who never see them do anything right but always see them when they are doing something wrong. More important, they begin to lose confidence in themselves.

The particular difficulty with educating inner-city children as opposed to middle-class children is that the middle-class child comes to school having been told a great deal about his role in school. The inner-city child, on the other hand, has to learn his role upon arrival in school. He needs to try out a variety of behaviors to find out which one is the one that gets him attention. We need to set up and define roles that will enable the child to attain the ends we have set out for him. We need, then, to support him with attention at any time he is playing the desired role.

The problem in an inner-city school where few know the correct role is that the teacher cannot interact with thirty children at the same time. In the early stages of learning a role, the child needs much more attention than he does later, when he has learned the role satisfactorily. It is here that the teacher of middle-class children has an easier time of it. Her children have more language for reading; her children come to school knowing that their job is to learn to read; many of her children have been in nursery school and have learned the game. In short, few of her children are totally ignorant of how they are to perform. Consequently, many of her children will continue to play the correct role because they need less attention to sustain them in the activities set out for them. This lack of knowledge about how to play the school role on the part of many inner-city children is why a smaller teacher-pupil or adult-pupil ratio is needed in the early grades of the inner-city school.

THE USE OF PARAPROFESSIONALS

The national teacher supply runs far behind the demand, and as with most other things, the supply for the inner-city is even more meager than the national supply. The solution is to use paraprofessionals selected from the inner-city and trained to do a specific job. The notion of paraprofessionals is a relatively new idea and the notion of teachers' aides isn't much older. The difficulty with the latter, however, is that their role is seen as marking papers, keeping records, and carrying out other non-teaching duties. This is no doubt beneficial to teachers and is certainly useful as a means of freeing teachers to plan and to think about their main task, teaching. It doesn't, however, respond to the problem of pupil-teacher ratio and increased attention for children.

The difficulty with the notions of how to use paraprofessionals is that a workable plan has not been found. Some are suggesting that they should be introduced to teaching at one level and involved more and more deeply in the role until they are functioning as full professionals. Our objection to this is that, to date, we have been by and large unsuccessful in our attempts to make college graduates with years of university training into successful professionals. If someone knows how to take high school graduates and/or high school dropouts and develop them into professional teachers, many colleges that train teachers would like to know about it. Many wouldn't. We doubt that it can be done without seriously undermining the definition of "professional" and without fostering a great deal more miseducation for the inner-city child. We propose, instead, to have the paraprofessional work with small groups of children in highly structured situations. Any given paraprofessional would be employed in only one part of the program — in either the reading phase or the mathematics or the language, etc. She would do her job under the closest supervision and only after appropriate training by her supervisor. Furthermore, the decision-making aspects of how to play the paraprofessional role would rest with the supervisor, not the trainee. To do it any other way is to ask the paraprofessional to be what she is not equipped to be, namely, a professional.

There are several advantages to this proposal. First, the adult-child ratio is brought down to a point where it is possible to give each child the attention he needs to develop an adequate self-concept. Second, the individual functioning as a paraprofessional is in a position to gain much personal satisfaction in a socially important occupation. Third, the fact that adults from the inner-city community are working with children in the schools helps define for these children the importance of school. Fourth, being given attention in the school role by a number of people is more beneficial to the child than being given attention by just one adult. Fifth, the use in the school of adults who go out into the inner-city community each evening will improve school-community relations, if the program is a good one. The very least it will do is to open up lines of communication between community and school. Sixth, the increased number of adults in the school will increase the opportunities that a child has to find a special friend — someone to whom he can talk, to whom he can relate, and with whom he can trade confidences that will be respected.

There are other consequences to our proposal. The regular teacher's role will be altered somewhat, and more supervisory help will be needed, as well as redefinition of the scope of present supervisory roles. The paraprofessionals will need to be taught the techniques of teaching in their area of the program, and they will need to be taught how to interact with children in a manner that emphasizes giving attention for desirable behavior in order to give consistent teaching throughout the school.

HOW SCHOOLS ENCOURAGE FAILURE

The authors have taught disadvantaged youngsters, emotionally disturbed youngsters, and a number of other types of children, all of whom had in common a failing academic record in school. In these situations, we have observed a number of phenomena that others have also observed, but from which many teachers will not learn. It might help to note these observations in order to support the validity of our principle in regard to giving attention to desired behavior.

OBSERVATION ONE

In going over the records of 14- to 18-year-olds who were in special classes and who had IQs ranging from 85 to 145, it was noted that each child had a "record" a mile long. Incidents of unacceptable behavior invariably went back to the early years of school. These students were punished in a variety of ways down through the years. Every time they did something "wrong," they were caught and punished. Now a school system that punishes a boy for ten years and has seen no change in the boy ought to conclude, if all reason hasn't deserted that school system, that there is something wrong with the way the boy is being handled. It should be evident that punishment doesn't work.

OBSERVATION TWO

Once a boy or girl is punished a couple of times, he gets a reputation (a self-concept) to which he feels he must live up. The teacher doesn't trust him. She watches him every minute. It's a game. The child's role isn't to learn to read. It's to outwit the teacher. The teacher's role isn't to teach reading. It's to catch the child in an illegal act. The battle is joined, with the child enlisting his peers and the teacher enlisting her peers. When the child enters school the following year, he may have spent the summer listening to his mother's attempts to convince him he was smart enough to be a success in school. He may even decide to try. But alas, the first day in class, a teacher new to the school says to the child, "Oh yes, I've heard about you. Well, young man, you won't get away with that nonsense in my class." The game is on again. The child is forced into the old role. The teacher watches his every move. If he does something a little out of line, the teacher lands all over him. If he observes that four other children were doing the same thing, she tells him that she's not worrying about them, because she knows that they know how to behave, even if he doesn't.

This is an example of some teachers' favorite logic trick: the self-confirming hypothesis. A variation of this is the reasoning that black children are stupid, stupid children can't learn, and if they can't learn there is no sense in teaching them. At the end of the school year the tests show that the black children didn't learn anything which, of course, proves that black children are stupid.

To return to our boy, let us merely note that the whole school, janitors and kitchen help included, seem to band together to give this child attention whenever he does something wrong. They then put it in his record so that the next time he does something wrong they can recite chapter and verse and prove they have been interested in helping him despite his uncooperative behavior. They even keep records to show his "progress." We know of one high school boy who was accused of an offense (many high schools have penal codes) of such magnitude that if convicted he could be permanently expelled. A hearing was held before the board of education. The boy, with an IQ of 140 and a better grasp than the school administration of the rules of evidence, proved his innocence. He was then expelled for his past record. In hearing his sentence and the reason for it, he observed that it didn't seem quite fair to expel him for alleged crimes, some ten years old, for which he had already been punished; but this legal nicety was overlooked by the board. The board reasoned that the boy obviously could not be helped in the schools. If the principal and assistant principal said he was bad, then he must be bad. Why would they lie?

Of course, they might be lying in order to protect themselves. If a couple of good teachers got together and encouraged the boy to do well and gave him attention for doing well, he might continue to do well. Someone might then ask: "Why couldn't the other teachers and the principal succeed with the boy? Are they incompetent?" Let someone build a school in the inner-city where the children learn, and that someone will be accused of doctoring the records. No one will be popular for having success with children where others have previously failed.

OBSERVATION THREE

Wherever a child has a long history of honest attention and praise, one sees a continued history of successes.

OBSERVATION FOUR

Wherever a child with a long history of failure does an about face, you can find an adult who came into that child's life just prior to the change in behavior and paid attention to the right things the child did and pretty much ignored the wrong things.

We conclude two things from the above observations. First, the 1½ million youngsters who drop out of school each year have had teachers who attended to what they did wrong, not to what they did right. Second, there is no excuse for it.

ENCOURAGING APPROPRIATE BEHAVIOR

It is not sufficient merely to demonstrate what happens when the opposite principle to the one we proposed is applied. Therefore, let us describe some situations in which our principle has been applied.

SITUATION ONE

A teacher is working with a class in which questions are being posed by the teacher, to be answered by the students. The expected role is that the children will raise their hands and speak when called upon. Edward continually yells out answers. The teacher ignores Edward. Edward continues to yell out answers, and the teacher continues to ignore him. Edward looks around and then starts raising his hand while continuing to yell out answers. The teacher still ignores him.

Mary says to Edward, as he looks at her in desperation, "It looks like you won't get called on as long as you keep yelling. He wants quiet."

For the next two questions, Edward raises his hand quietly. The second time he does this, the teacher calls on him. During the rest of the lesson, with one exception when he forgets, Edward quietly raises his hand when he wishes to offer an answer. The following day, Edward starts out by shouting again but quickly alters his behavior to the accepted pattern when he is again ignored.

SITUATION TWO

Louisa is a daydreamer. In the daily twenty-minute, independent work period, when the student role is to read quietly, study an assignment, or find some other "school work" on which they feel they need to work, Louisa spends her time daydreaming, walking around the room, or generally pestering others in the room. The teacher's strategy has always been to reprimand Louisa or to gently suggest that there must be something she needs to study. Occasionally, the teacher would find some work for her, and Louisa would work as long as the teacher stayed with her. However, soon after the teacher moved on, Louisa would go back to her desultory activities. One Monday, the teacher ignored Louisa's daydreaming during the independent study period. Getting no reaction, Louisa began moving about the room, directing brief glances toward the teacher. Tuesday, the same thing happened, and when Louisa daydreamed her way through arithmetic and social studies, the teacher continued to ignore her. Tuesday afternoon, Louisa participated actively in the science lesson, and the teacher called on her and on two occasions smiled at her. Wednesday, during the independent study period, Louisa began working on her arithmetic assignment. The teacher walked over, quietly examined Louisa's work, smiled, and moved on to the next child. When Louisa left for lunch, the teacher commented on how well she had worked that morning. Louisa said, "You know I didn't waste one minute today." The teacher said, "Yes, and your work was rather well done."

SITUATION THREE

Phyllis was a second grader who was rather a social isolate. This was particularly noticeable on the playground during free play, when Phyllis was frequently left to play completely alone. Her popularity was not increased by her habit of playing "tattle-tale" and reporting to the teacher each slight misdemeanor of the other children, such as, "Johnny just went down the slide backwards."

The teacher decided to try to decrease Phyllis' tattling and to increase her interaction with other children. Her procedure for accomplishing this was to ignore the tales Phyllis told and to look away from Phyllis while she was telling them. Whenever Phyllis was playing with another child, the teacher came over to them and joined in the group. If Phyllis went back to playing alone, the teacher moved away from Phyllis and from the group. The teacher approached Phyllis and her playmates regardless of whether Phyllis had begun the group play or some other child had come up to Phyllis. In this way, Phyllis was reinforced for playing with other children, and the other children were reinforced for playing with Phyllis.

Within a two-week period, Phyllis doubled the amount of time she spent interacting with others on the playground, and her tattling dropped to almost nothing.

SITUATION FOUR

Danny was a kindergartner who loved to play with clay and blocks, who hated to help put away the blocks at cleanup time, and who periodically got into fist fights with two other boys in the class. The teacher wanted Danny to learn to cooperate at cleanup time and to avoid fighting in school.

The teacher felt the fighting was a serious matter, since Danny and the other boys were in some danger of being hurt in the pummeling they did. Scolding the boys for fighting would be giving them attention for their misbehavior, but ignoring them while they hit each other would increase the danger of someone getting hurt. The answer seemed to be to isolate the boys from each other whenever a fight occurred. This prevented them from fighting and also from receiving attention. The isolation was *not* preceded or followed by a "talking to" from the teacher. The fighting diminished and eventually ceased.

In encouraging Danny to clean up the blocks, the teacher took another tack. On a day when Danny stowed a few blocks away in the proper bins, she said, "I'm glad to see you helped clean up the blocks today. Would you like to play with clay for a few minutes while we get ready for a snack?" This approach was repeated whenever Danny put away the blocks. The more blocks he put away, the longer he was allowed to play with the clay.

Gradually the pattern of putting away blocks became normal behavior for Danny. The teacher then began to decrease the clay time from every day to every other day and, finally, to once or twice a week. Danny continued to put away the blocks whenever he played with them.

The foregoing situations illustrate some important aspects of the principle of attending to desired behavior. First, in addition to rewarding desirable behavior and ignoring undesirable behavior, it is sometimes necessary to *isolate* a child for unacceptable behavior — that is, for behavior that is dangerous to himself or to others. This isolation does not violate the principle if the child is not receiving attention from others during the isolation period. Putting a child out in the hall or sending him to the principal's office is not generally effective isolation, since he will probably receive a good deal of attention from passersby in both these settings. An unobtrusive corner of the room, out of sight of peers, would make a better "isolation booth," and the isolation period should not be too prolonged.

Second, the reward for desirable behavior need not always be the attention of the teacher. Anything to which the child responds positively can serve as a reward. Thus, art or craft periods, singing periods, listening to records or stories, or free time can conceivably be used as rewards for desirable classroom behavior. With inner-city children, in some instances food has been used as a highly effective reward. Small snacks of nutritious food can thus serve a dual purpose, improving the child's health and helping him to learn socially acceptable behavior at the same time.

Note that the reward is given after the desired action is performed. In none of the above situations does the teacher say, "If you do such and such, then I will let you have a play period." The latter is bribery. We are not interested in bribing children.

Third, the reward for desirable behavior needs to be used consistently in the beginning; that is, the child must be rewarded *every time* he performs the desired behavior until the pattern of behavior is well established or has become a habit. The reward then can be used less frequently and eventually only on rare occasions. The desired behavior will be maintained without the reward.

This aspect of applying the principle of attending to desired behavior is one that becomes extremely difficult, if not impossible, in a classroom with one adult and thirty children. It can, however, be rather easily used in a classroom where each adult works with a small group of children at a time. In this setting, the adult can concentrate on one or two children for a week or two, then as the desired patterns of behavior become established, he can shift attention to another child in the group. As indicated earlier, this is a strong reason for the use of paraprofessionals in the inner-city classroom.

Fourth, the principle of attending to desired behavior focuses upon affecting the *social* behavior of the child. It is not a method of "brainwashing," and is not suggested here as a means of affecting the child's thinking. The fact is that no social group can function effectively unless most of its members follow certain agreed-upon rules. Every social group uses some method of encouraging its members to follow these rules. Law enforcement is one such method. Giving a raise in pay or a job promotion is another such method.

All teachers attempt to get children to play the accepted role in school. Maintaining discipline is a crucial part of the teacher's job. It is a part of the job that has not been too effectively handled in the past, or there would not be so much professional and public concern about it.

What is being suggested here is that the principle of attending to desired behavior is a more effective way of helping the child to learn more rapidly the role of the student in the classroom setting. It has the additional value of emphasizing the child's positive actions, thus helping him to achieve a positive self-concept. These seem to be powerful reasons for applying the principle in the teaching of children in the inner-city school.

We do not suggest application of this method as a means of influencing a child's cognitive behavior. In the cognitive realm we are interested in developing the child's ability to think for himself and to test and evaluate his own thinking. This goal cannot be accomplished by having the teacher decide what answers are correct. Furthermore, we are interested in increasing the self-rewarding qualities of problem-solving activity. Children who learn to think for themselves also learn that thinking is its own reward. The teacher who continually rewards correct answers interferes with this self-motivation. If the child's purpose for thinking is to please the teacher, then his intellectual activity will diminish sharply when he leaves school. This is not an educational goal we wish to pursue.

There are other factors that go into developing positive self-concepts. These have to do with the kinds of activities in which the child engages, the pedagogical strategies of the child's teachers, the classroom environment, and the successes the child has along the way. These factors will be dealt with throughout the following chapters.

In the chapter on administration, we shall take up the problem of training those who work with the children in the use of behavior-modification procedures. For the moment, we wish merely to establish the importance of behavior-modification principles and procedures as a means of developing positive self-concepts and to establish that, in our view, the process of developing positive self-concepts is of sufficient importance to require that all activities and procedures need to be analyzed in terms of their impact upon self-concepts.

THREE: CHARTING A NEW CURRICULUM COURSE

The presentation of a rationale for a program in an inner-city school will be of value to urban educators only if the theoretical foundations can be translated into curriculum practice. We shall deal in some detail with the question of the curriculum in the chapters that follow this one. In this chapter we should like to give the reader an overview of a sample primary program and suggest some problems that must be handled if the program is to succeed. This overview will take the form of a daily schedule, since this enables the reader quickly to note the organization of time for students, teachers, para-professionals, and other personnel. In addition, some general curriculum considerations, such as the use of centers, trips, and scholarship weeks, will be discussed.

The preschool and kindergarten programs are fairly consistent with the traditional organization and will be dealt with in detail in Chapter 5; we shall not deal with them here other than to note that they are 5-hour programs rather than 3-hour programs and that they use paraprofessionals. The first-grade schedule is planned for ninety-six children in four rooms, which we might label 101, 102, 103, and 104. Each room has a regularly assigned teacher who has been certified by the state. The school day runs from 8:15 A.M. to 2:30 P.M. The schedule is blocked out below. Inside the parentheses, we have indicated who has the major responsibility for children during the indicated time period. T denotes teacher, PP denotes paraprofessional, TA denotes teachers' aide, and PTA denotes an activity handled by the Parent-Teacher Association.

	Room 101	Room 102	Room 103	Room 104
8:15 – 8:30	Attendance (T)			
8:30 – 9:00	Reading (PP)	Math (PP)	Language (T)	Language (T)
9:05 – 9:35	Ind. Read. (T)	Ind. Math (T)	Reading (PP)	Math (PP)
9:40 – 9:55	Snack (PTA)			
10:00 – 10:30	Math (PP)	Reading (PP)	Ind. Read. (T)	Ind. Math (T)
10:35 – 11:05	Ind. Math (T)	Ind. Read. (T)	Math (PP)	Reading (PP)
11:10 – 11:30	Play Period			
11:30 – 12:00	Language (T)	Language (T)	Ind. Math (T)	Ind. Read. (T)
12:00 – 12:40	Lunch (PTA)			
12:40 – 2:30	Uncommon Learning Centers			

Examining the above schedule in a little more detail, we find the teachers greeting the children at 8:15 A.M. and taking attendance in all four classrooms. At 8:30 A.M., the children in Room 101 are broken down into four groups and meet with four paraprofessionals who will teach them to read. Class 102 also breaks down into four groups and meets with four other paraprofessionals for instruction in mathematics. The regular teachers of these two classrooms observe the children at work with the paraprofessionals. The supervisors travel with the teachers and observe the paraprofessionals.

One problem becomes evident here. That is that the group work, as outlined, requires eight teaching stations, and only two classrooms are available. This problem is solvable, and we shall return to it in the chapter on administration. From 8:30 to 9 A.M., classrooms 103 and 104 are with their regular teachers receiving language arts instruction. At 9 A.M., the children in 101 and 102 return to their classrooms and work independently, in pairs, or in small groups, consolidating what they had in class the previous half hour. The regular classroom teacher is with them and gives assistance, special instructions, and other aids to learning based on her observation of the children's performance in their group work with the paraprofessionals. Classrooms 103 and 104 are at this time working, in groups of six, on reading or mathematics with the paraprofessionals.

We have placed snack time at 9:40 A.M. on the assumption that some children may have had inadequate breakfasts. We are of the opinion that PTA monies ought to be used for snacks for the children, rather than for plaques or television sets. The menu for snack time ought to be milk and something nutritious—custard, for example. We also feel that the children and the teachers might well be separated at this time, and we therefore recommend that snack time be supervised by the PTA. This serves four purposes. One, it increases the opportunity for communication between parents and school; two, it involves the parents in an essential school activity; three, it gives teachers a break for coffee which tends to refresh; four, it gives teachers, paraprofessionals, and supervisors a chance to swap notes.

From 10 to 11:05 A.M., the reading and mathematics program is continued in the manner described above, with those who have earlier received instruction in mathematics now getting instruction in reading, and those who have had reading instruction now receiving instruction in mathematics.

At 11:05 A.M., the children have a play period in the room or outdoors with the teacher. Many games are possible at this time. We suggest games that involve some mild exercise.

At 11:05 A.M., the paraprofessionals are through working with the children for the morning. From 11:05 A.M. until 12:30 P.M., they will meet with the supervisor to discuss their teaching and the curriculum, and they will have lunch and prepare for the afternoon work in the uncommon learning centers or with the second graders.

The children will complete the morning in the room with the classroom teacher, working in language arts or independent mathematics or reading.

At 12:00 noon, the children will go to lunch. We recommend that the lunchroom have some attractive paintings and/or art reprints around the room. We recommend that music (not too loud) be played. We recommend that children be allowed to talk. We recommend that they be allowed freedom to go to the bathroom if it is required and that they be allowed to do so without first asking permission. We recommend that those supervising do so in a relaxed manner. We recommend that every time a tray is dropped it should be picked up without a lot of screaming. We recommend that parents sit at tables and talk with the children. We recommend that, if lunch can be finished comfortably in less than forty minutes, lunch period be shortened.

At 12:40, the children will go to the center of their choice until dismissal time at 2:30 P.M.

THE UNCOMMON LEARNING CENTERS

Centers, as we conceive of them, will have the following characteristics. Children will attend the center of their choice, switching from center to center as they see fit. They may attend a center for a month or two as a regular and then attend another center. A child may, if he wishes, spend forty minutes in one center and then spend an hour in another each day. Each center would be manned by at least one adult. This adult may be a teacher, a paraprofessional, a member of the community, a college student, or a high school student. Each center would have its own activity, which would set it apart from the other centers. Some possible centers would be the following: an arts and craft center; a music center in which the children would learn to play instruments (an offshoot of this center might be a band); a story center in which children would hear and learn to tell stories or to read poems (a choral speaking group might grow out of this center); a reading center for pleasure reading; a mathematics center where various mathematical questions that have occurred to students may be pursued; a doll center where the children can make dolls and dresses and then dress their dolls; a dance center. In the second grade, we would add a repair center where bikes and other toys could be repaired by the children, a creative language center, an acting center, a photography center, a science center, and a sewing and cooking center.

Space limitations may necessitate that some of these centers be located off, but near, the school grounds. Others, however, by their very nature, suggest where they should be located. In some instances, more than one room may be needed for a particular center, or more than one adult may be needed in a large center. In some of the centers, first and second graders could work together during part of the afternoon.

The function of these centers is to involve the child in an activity that he enjoys and in which he will learn skills and develop self-confidence. The center is a place where one develops interests, makes friends with others who have similar interests, and discusses anything and everything with those friends. It is a place where interests cultivated outside the school are brought into the school to be developed and furthered, and where other interests are cultivated and developed that may be carried on outside of school. A center is a relaxing place where the child learns lessons in responsibility, cooperation, and pride because it belongs to him and his peers. It is a place where he can be unique. It is a place where he can define and solve problems that arise out of his self-direction and interests, and not out of a teacher's direction or interest.

The function of the adult in the center is to help the child resolve difficulties he may face, to help him find materials, and to generally guide him toward seeing the possibilities that exist in pursuing the activity further.

As the uncommon learning centers progress, some will remain essentially centers where individuals work as individuals, while others will tend to lead to group activity, from time to time, on a slightly more structured basis. The dance center may lead to a group performance. The repair center, on the other hand, will tend to remain individual and short-lived in nature for most children, though one or two children may spend much of their time there repairing other children's toys.

Uncommon learning centers may well combine their energies to accomplish a mutual goal. The dance and music group might get together in order

24

to put on a show. The cooking center might prepare and serve part of a buffet for the PTA, with decorations made by the arts and craft center. The photography center might work with the mathematics and science centers on a display.

The uncommon learning centers we have suggested are not the full range of possibilities. What centers a school has depends on the talents of its staff and upon others whom the school can interest in participating. The problem of staff, the economics of centers, and a number of related matters will be discussed in the chapter on administration.

The rules that guide how the centers will run are as follows:
1. Be flexible.
2. Encourage the children to try a number of centers.
3. Final selection of the center in which he will work is always the child's.
4. Use behavior-modification techniques to teach acceptable behavior in the centers.
5. Allow children a significant role in establishing what constitutes acceptable behavior in the center.
6. The decision as to whether a center is to participate in scholarship week (to be discussed later in this chapter) rests with individuals in the center.
7. Centers are places in which children are to be doing and thinking, not listening to adults give speeches.
8. New centers will rise out of the desires of the children.

FIELD TRIPS

As the children work in each center, they may find that the confines of the school are limiting and decide on a trip that they believe will be helpful. Thus, the children in the art center may arrange a trip to a museum. The children in the photography center may take a trip to a photographer's studio or to a magazine or newspaper plant.

These trips should be open to all children, with the currently active members having first choice. We suggest the following guidelines for trips:
1. Groups should be relatively small, with no more than sixteen children going on any one trip.
2. There should be at least one adult for each four children. Draw on the PTA.
3. Trips should be planned and organized by the children as much as possible.
4. Specific purpose and goals of the trip should be agreed upon.
5. Photographs and/or films should be made during the trip.
6. Discussions should follow the trip. The films and photographs can be used to focus discussion and reinforce learning.
7. Most trips should be afternoon affairs and should not infringe on morning studies.
8. Children should be given ten "chits" on October first of each year and be able to use one as a ticket for each trip they wish to take.

9. If, after a trip, you ask a child, "What did you learn today?" and he replies, "We had a good time," then something is wrong with your trips.

As we envision these trips, as many as one hundred trips will be taken by first graders and one hundred more by second graders each year. Almost without exception, they will be within ten miles of the school, and many will be within walking distance. The function of the trips is to expand the child's environment by letting him see the city physically, by letting him see men at work. The trips can provide lessons in economics, geography, social behavior, language, human relations, arithmetic, reading, and everything else. Since each child has ten chits, he has to make decisions: "Should I spend a chit to go to the museum, which doesn't interest me except for the subway ride, or should I save it to go to the bicycle-repair center, which really interests me but is only down the block?" With ten chits the child can, of course, squander a few and make a few errors in judgment. Sometimes an error in judgment may lead to a new interest: "I went for the bus ride but came home interested in art."

SCHOLARSHIP WEEK

The trips that flow naturally from the activities of the centers also are useful for presenting opportunities for developing skills necessary for scholarship week. In proposing a scholarship week, we are proposing that twice a year the first and second grades present a scholarship week. This should go on two or three afternoons and one evening and should be a showcase for the children and their work.

Scholarship weeks serve several functions. First, they are a vehicle for bringing parents and others in the community into contact with the school. Second, they are a means by which the school can identify useful talent in the community that might contribute to the program. Third, they give an additional social purpose to children's activity. Fourth, they provide an opportunity for the child to demonstrate the progress he has been making. Fifth, the praise that comes from people outside the school for a job well done enhances the self-concept and affirms that the student role is worthwhile and is supported by the community. Sixth, scholarship week brings parents and teachers together at a positive moment. Seventh, scholarship week is a chance to bring a number of separate activities together so that the child begins to develop an appreciation of how the curriculum hangs together.

Let us elaborate briefly on some of the above. We are assuming that in building an outstanding educational institution in the inner-city the staff hired for that purpose will be insufficient and that the monies allocated to the school will also be insufficient. The solution requires not only the ideas necessary for an outstanding program, but also the active support of the community in which the school exists. It is not sufficient that the community be friendly. It is necessary for the community to be actively involved. Some few in the community will be active with only an idea to start them. The rest, however, will need to see some signs of progress. They will also need to be convinced that they are really wanted by the school. Once you can do this, many more members of the community will join you. One way to show the community what is being accomplished is by having a scholarship week. Those who come will report what they see back to the others. Some who come to see will ask questions, some will make suggestions, some will tell you it "ain't education," and some will say, "I hear you need help. May I be of assistance?" In any event, a school that will put its product on display eliminates the charge that it is locking the public out. A school that puts on an honest display that has quality will win support. A large segment of the inner-city community knows what good education means to them and will support it when it comes. The rest will come to learn what a good education means.

We see scholarship week as flowing in large part from the centers. We see children giving verbal reports about their displays, serving food, playing host, giving demonstrations, performing, acting as guides, etc. Each of these roles requires skills that must be learned. The children must anticipate what will be called for and then prepare. After scholarship week, they will need to evaluate the show to see what was handled effectively and what could be improved.

While scholarship week is seen as flowing in large part from the centers, it is also an opportunity for the children to describe how they are learning reading and mathematics. Scholarship week then becomes an additional reason for examining how we learn, so that we may describe the program to the parents. Demonstrations can be given on word-attack skills, mathematical thinking, etc.

One of the chief functions of scholarship week is to create a situation that requires the community to come into the school and to look at what is going on. By having the children actively participating, they are on hand to see the public when it comes. The result is that the children see that what they are doing as students has social significance, is applauded by the community, and is seen by the community as being relevant. Some who come will be strangers to the children, and the children in their several roles will have to deal with these strangers. The children will hear the strangers commenting about the work, the demonstrations, and the displays. And they will learn a little about critics. They will be hurt a little by some careless remark, and they may swell with pride over the strangers' compliments. They may resolve, "As good a job as we did this time—next time we'll do better."

We make one strong recommendation in setting up scholarship week. Make it the kind of affair that is childlike. Be honest. Don't show just the best displays. Don't have only the best talkers giving presentations. That the week is a show, we don't deny. That the preparation is a learning experience is of greater importance. The actual week itself is meant to be both a learning experience and a culmination to other learning experiences. We once knew a child who was part of a presentation that required four weeks of work before this child could make an eight-line presentation. It was successful, and he talked of that moment for months. He was 14, and his performance wasn't a great one by most standards, but it was his performance, and he pulled it off, much to his own surprise. He did it despite tremendous fears of failure, and in doing it he demonstrated to his audience that he was capable of learning. He had in this presentation one little moment of success in the academic world. We can't help wondering why he couldn't have had dozens of such successes in his many years in school.

Scholarship week must not teach hypocrisy. It must be honest. It must meet the standards the children set. Its success must give them honest pride in what they accomplished. Pride will lead to higher standards. Children quickly learn and accept that when you set your goals higher you must work harder. They also learn that with the increased efforts often come increased rewards.

We are not suggesting in the above that the children be simply told, "Here, it's your show. You develop it." They'll need help and advice and suggestions and support. If the job is done honestly, the public will see it and appreciate that children and staff worked hard together to make it a job well done. The children will see it as well, and the bonds between staff and students will be that much closer.

THE SECOND-GRADE SCHEDULE

Earlier in the chapter, we laid out the schedule for ninety-six children in the four first grades. The staff included four teachers, eight paraprofessionals, two teachers' aides, a supervisor, and PTA members. We should now like to lay out the second-grade schedule for ninety-six children in six groups. Each classroom has sixteen children, a teacher, a paraprofessional, and one-third of a teachers' aide.

	I	II	III	IV	V	VI
8:15 — 8:30	———————————— Attendance ————————————					
8:30 — 9:25	Reading	Reading	Math	Math	Language	Language
9:25 — 9:45	———————————— Snack ————————————					
9:45 — 10:40	Language	Language	Reading	Reading	Math	Math
10:40 — 11:10	———————————— Play Period ————————————					
11:10 — 12:00	Math	Math	Language	Language	Reading	Reading
12:00 — 12:40	———————————— Lunch ————————————					
12:40 — 1:30	———— Small-Group, Tutorial, and Independent Work ————					
1:30 — 3:00	———————— Uncommon Learning Centers ————————					

The schedules for each class are slightly different to accommodate the library. The second-grade reading program, which is described in Chapter 9, is in large part an individualized reading program and necessitates using the library. By distributing the reading schedule over the morning, the library isn't deluged with young readers. The mathematics program is described in Chapter 7, and the language arts program is described in Chapter 11.

The afternoon is started with what is labeled as small-group, tutorial, independent work. The independent work, while intended for all, is primarily for those students who have done exceptionally well. Children will differ in how much they will have accomplished in two years of schooling and seven years of living, and the better the school, the greater will be the differences. Some children will have had perceptual difficulties that were resolved later than others. Some will have taken to reading or language studies like a duck takes to water, while others may have started slower and progressed more slowly. The slowest of students, under the reading, mathematics, and language curriculum we will propose, should be on grade level by the end of the first grade. Others will be higher — some as high as the fourth- and fifth-grade levels. We feel, however, that being on grade level is not sufficient and should not continue. Therefore, we propose that from 12:40 to 1:30 P.M. the six teachers of the second grade and the eight paraprofessionals from the first grade should work extensively with these children. If thirty-six children can handle independent work, a staff of twenty is left to deal with the remaining sixty and should be able to move them along. We shall say more about how this is done in the chapter on administration. We merely wish to note here that any success that didn't come in the first grade must come in the second grade, before a pattern of mediocrity sets in as a way of life.

SUMMARY

The thrust of this chapter has been to offer a view of what a school day would look like in our first and second grades for 192 students. The children engage in two different kinds of activities. The first we might label teacher-structured activities, in which the child is given experiences set up by the teacher to enable the child to more fully develop reading, mathematical, and language skills. The second we might label student-structured activities, in which the child pursues activities that he feels are significant and productive. The two are related, for in the student-structured activities the child will often use skills learned in the teacher-structured activities. In some circumstances, skills learned in the student-structured activities can apply in the teacher-structured situation. Sometimes the two will be directly related, as in the instance of a second-grade child in his individualized reading program reading a book on the dance for his work in the dance center.

Out of the teacher-structured situations, but much more often out of the centers or student-structured situations, trips will evolve that will expand the world of the children.[1] These trips will relate directly to the student-structured

[1] All learning experiences that involve a student and a teacher have both a component that is teacher-structured and a component that is student-structured. We have drawn the distinction we have here to indicate that in the first type the burden of responsibility for setting up the activity and deciding what is to be done lies with the teacher. In the student-structured situation, the child has more of this responsibility.

situations in almost every instance. They will also relate to the teacher-structured situations in many instances, particularly to the language program.

The fourth component we have laid out in our program is the scholarship week, which is seen as an extension of the first three components and which serves the function of unifying the curriculum for the child and displaying the work of the school to the community.

FOUR: DEVELOPING PERCEPTUAL ABILITIES

In kindergarten and first grade, many children are now able to use their bodies and their senses in a coordinated, integrated fashion, which in turn helps them to deal with the world as a predictable, familiar, and manageable entity. The child now has a vast background of knowledge and experience in terms of manipulating objects with his hands while looking at them; he has learned to turn his head and to tell from what direction various sounds are coming; he can orient and position himself in relation to various objects in his world so that he can manipulate these objects in a successful manner. He visually observes characteristics and features of many objects in his world and is able to note the relationship between similar and different objects.

The period of maximum perceptual growth and development in children progresses from the age of $3\frac{1}{2}$ to approximately 7 or 8. Some children begin to lag in their perceptual development, and they soon suffer from a number of handicaps. They find the world and its objects unpredictable, confusing, unrecognizable, and unreliable. These children are often impulsive, distractible, clumsy, and inept in tasks and sports. They become angry, emotionally upset, and confused because of their difficulty in coping; and this in turn leads to lowered self-confidence or emotional disturbance. Often, children prefer not to try new tasks rather than to risk failure or confusion.

Various studies have shown that approximately 20 percent of children in the early elementary grades have some kind of lag in their development that can be called a perceptual deficiency. As a consequence, it has also been found that when children suffer from such a developmental lag there is a predictable difficulty in school in the content areas of reading, writing, and arithmetic. The causes for deficiencies in perceptual development are often difficult to explain. It is possible, however, that these lags in development can be caused by physiological factors that occur during pregnancy, during birth, or after birth. These conditions may not originate from the sense organs themselves: the messages that are sent from the eye to the brain and the resulting connections of different parts of the brain with each other may not occur each and every time in a predictable manner. This inability may cause the following response to occur: the child finds himself reacting differently to the same stimulus without understanding that he has encountered it before or without remembering the correct response that he must make.

There are many ways of determining whether children do have some type of perceptual deficiency. The teacher can evaluate the effectiveness of the child's performance as he copes with academic material. Children who cannot reliably and consistently decode the same words time after time may have difficulty in understanding the directions in which the symbols or letters go. For instance, the only difference between a "b" and a "d" is the direction of the half circle on the bottom of the vertical line. The difference between the words "saw" and "was" is the sequential arrangement of three letters. If the image that the child sees tells him that the letters in the word "was" are "s-a-w," he is going to respond on the basis of this information. He may or may not recognize that there was an error in the way in which he perceived the word. When the teacher informs the child that the word was read incorrectly, he becomes unsure of his ability to see things in an objective, accurate manner.

The child who cannot understand various kinds of spatial positions, such as *up* and *down, behind, in front, left* and *right*, becomes confused when he has to utilize these concepts when dealing with objects outside of himself, such as symbols or numbers. Children have to understand relationships between objects, and they may become confused when attempting to explain these relationships accurately. For instance, a series of letters such as in the word "glove" may be arranged "glvoe" or "golve." Sometimes a child can recognize a certain symbol, letter, or word in one context, but when the size, color, or background is changed, he does not perceive it as being familiar and reacts as if it were a new and novel object. The recognition that a particular object has been encountered before may not help him at another time if the object is put into a novel situation. Some children have difficulty in differentiating the most important aspects of objects to which they are attending from what should properly be considered background or incidental features. These children cannot sort out the essential from the unessential, and thereby become confused and disorganized in terms of the responses they make. The difficulties encountered by the child in all these areas may be brought into play when he attempts to reproduce symbols when writing letters or numbers. He may spend much of his attention or energy attempting to spell correctly, thereby losing much of the meaning of that to which he should be attending because of the overemphasis on sheer mechanics.

TESTING

The classroom teacher needs certain prerequisite knowledge in order to understand, evaluate, and meaningfully diagnose the student's level of perceptual functioning. Such knowledge should include understanding the various components of perception, such as levels of motor functioning, spatial orientation, levels of integration in the visual and other sensory-motor areas, form discrimination, and the indirect components of perception that involve language, cognition, and social and emotional development. This knowledge should be meaningfully translated so that, by observing and working with children, the teacher can pinpoint levels of development or areas of deficiency. A systematic approach to evaluation of children is through a check list, with scoring keys that can be used to delineate possible problem areas. This approach allows for quantification in order that scores can be tallied across problem areas, and mean or average scores can be obtained. The procedure also allows for re-evaluation after specific time periods have elapsed, at which time the degree of progress that has been achieved can be substantiated for analysis. Such an approach allows for experimental or research possibilities, and the teacher then has data at her disposal for suggesting modifications in curriculum or educational theory.

GROSS MOTOR MOVEMENTS

1. Walking board

Rationale: The usefulness of the walking board is that it dramatically illustrates the child's ability to balance and to employ the postural flexibility that he or she has achieved. Several other concepts are also illustrated, such as spatial orientation, laterality, and generalization to other activities on the board.

Equipment: A 2- by 4-inch board, 10 or 12 feet long.

Procedure: Instruct the child to walk on the board in his bare feet. He should first walk forwards on the board, with body erect and eyes focused on an

33

object or a mark that is at eye level on the wall. Next, he should walk backwards on the board. He should then be instructed to walk sideways up the board and then to return again in the sideways position.

Evaluation: The child's performance can be evaluated on a 4-point scale.

1A. Balance: forward movement.
   0. The child cannot maintain balance on the board.
   1. The child has poor balance in that he steps off the board several times.
   2. The child loses his balance but can regain it.
   3. The child walks easily without losing his balance.

1B. Balance: backward movement.
   0. The child cannot maintain balance on the board.
   1. The child has poor balance in that he steps off the board several times.
   2. The child loses his balance but can regain it.
   3. The child walks easily without losing his balance.

1C. Balance: sideways movement.
   0. The child cannot maintain balance on the board.
   1. The child has poor balance in that he steps off the board several times.
   2. The child loses his balance but can regain it.
   3. The child walks easily without losing his balance.

1D. Coordination: forward movement.
   0. The child's movements are jerky, uneven, and uncorrectable, so that he cannot remain on the board.
   1. The child's movements are jerky, uneven, and he attempts to walk rapidly or extremely slowly to control his body. He steps off the board several times.
   2. The child's movements are uneven, and he has to search for those movements and positions that maintain his position on the board.
   3. The child's movements are smooth and even, and he easily and deliberately moves across the board.

1E. Coordination: backward movement.
   0. The child's movements are jerky, uneven, and uncorrectable, so that he cannot remain on the board.
   1. The child's movements are jerky, uneven, and he attempts to walk rapidly or extremely slowly to control his body. He steps off the board several times.
   2. The child's movements are uneven, and he has to search for those movements and positions that maintain his position on the board.
   3. The child's movements are smooth and even, and he easily and deliberately moves across the board.

1F. Coordination: sideways movement.
   0. The child's movements are jerky, uneven, and uncorrectable, so that he cannot remain on the board.

1. The child's movements are jerky, uneven, and he attempts to walk rapidly or extremely slowly to control his body. He steps off the board several times.
2. The child's movements are uneven, and he has to search for those movements and positions that maintain his position on the board.
3. The child's movements are smooth and even, and he easily and deliberately moves across the board.

2. Jumping, hopping, skipping, and balance

Rationale: These activities are useful in observing how children use large muscle groups that also involve balance, laterality, rhythmic development, and control.

Equipment: None.

Procedure:

2A. Jumping with two feet together. The child is instructed to jump several times and travel across the room, keeping his feet together.

2B. Jumping with one foot at a time, keeping his feet together. The child is instructed to have one foot off the floor and to take jumps on the other foot. The feet are then alternated.

Evaluation:

0. Child cannot jump with feet together.
1. Child jumps, using left or right side of body.
2. Hesitations, false starts, and alternations during jumps.
3. Child jumps smoothly and evenly, showing coordination.

Hopping

2C. Hopping once right/left. The child is instructed to hop once on his right foot and once on his left foot.

2D. Hopping twice right/left. The child is instructed to hop twice on his right foot and twice on his left foot.

2E. Hopping twice right/left once. The child is instructed to hop twice on his right foot and once on his left foot.

2F. Hopping twice left/right once. The child is instructed to hop twice on his left foot and once on his right foot.

2G. Hopping once right/left holding on to desk. This activity is for those children who cannot perform tasks 2C, 2D, 2E, and 2F adequately. The children are to hold on to a desk to maintain balance and control.

Evaluation:

0. The child cannot maintain balance; shows wild, uncontrolled movements.
1. Poor balance; movements uneven and moves radically from spot.
2. Lack of rhythm in alternating; shifts with hesitation.
3. Shows rhythm in alternating; shifts without hesitation.

Skipping:

2H.   Skipping. The child is instructed to skip across the room and back.

Evaluation:

    0.   Cannot skip.
    1.   Jerky, uneven; leaves out parts of movements, such as the slight hop.
    2.   Movements uncoordinated and mechanical.
    3.   Skips rhythmically and evenly across the room.

Balance

2I.   The children are instructed to extend one foot 10 inches to the side, extend the arm on the same side and hold it out straight, and maintain a straight posture for ten seconds with their eyes closed. The examiner counts aloud. Repeat on the other side. The children then repeat this procedure with their eyes open.

Evaluation:

    0.   Cannot balance.
    1.   Cannot maintain position, but touches foot to floor or wobbles actively.
    2.   Balance maintained for only a short time, with exaggerated recovery.
    3.   Balances without difficulty.

3.   Imitation of Body Parts and Their Location

Rationale: An evaluation of this knowledge determines the degree to which a child has an appreciation of his body image, the parts of his body, their names, and their location.

Procedure: The child is told, "Do what I do." The examiner then does the following:

1.   Touches both hands to his shoulders.
2.   Touches both hands to his hips.
3.   Touches both hands to his knees.
4.   Touches both hands to his ankles.
5.   Raises his right hand to his right shoulder.
6.   Raises his left hand straight over his head.
7.   Touches his right shoulder with his left hand.
8.   Touches his left eye with his left forefinger.

Evaluation: The child is observed to determine whether he can accurately imitate the movements and positions of the examiner. This procedure is useful for children who may not have learned to identify with labels parts of their bodies. The child is then asked to follow through with the instructions as noted below.

36

3A. Identification of body parts and their locations

Procedure: The child is instructed to stand in front of the examiner at the distance of 8 feet. He is told:

1. Touch your shoulders
2. Touch your hips
      head
      ankles
      ears
      feet
      eyes
      elbows
      mouth
3. Raise your left hand
4. Raise your right hand
5. Put your left hand on your left ear
6. Put your right hand on your left shoulder
7. Put your left hand on your right knee
8. Put your right hand on your left elbow

Evaluation: This procedure determines, first, if the child appears to recognize the names of the body parts and can accurately touch these parts when asked to do so. Secondly, it determines whether he is able to differentiate left from right and whether he can cross the midline at those times when he is asked to cross from left to right or from right to left. If the child appears initially to understand where his left hand is and then seems to forget, and it is necessary to ask him again in the examination in order to determine whether he really knows what is left or right, it was guesswork on his part.

 0. Child follows examiner with hesitation and mistakes; he cannot locate parts on his own body.
 1. Child uses only one side of his body. He confuses left and right and does not know the parts of his body.
 2. Child knows body parts and can differentiate between left and right, but not consistently.
 3. Child knows parts of his body and the left-right sequence.

FORM PERCEPTION

In the area of form perception, the emphasis is on the child's ability to reproduce geometric forms in an organized and accurate manner. This activity shows the developmental level of eye-hand motor skills, directional and pursuit movements, and organizational abilities having to do with perceptual maturity. The Copy Forms, initially used by Arnold L. Gesell,[1] are seven geometric forms — circle, cross, square, triangle, divided triangle, horizontal diamond, and vertical diamond — that the children are asked to copy. R. G.

[1] A. Gesell, F. L. Ilg, and G. E. Bullis, *Vision: Its Development in Infant and Child*, New York, Paul B. Hocker, 1941.

Lowder examined 1510 school children in Winter Haven, Florida, and found a significant relationship between perceptual ability and school achievement.[2]

Equipment: Seven geometric figures mounted individually on 3- by 5-inch cards, a sheet of unlined, 8½- by 11-inch paper, and sharpened pencils.

Procedure: The child is seated at a desk. Each copy form is presented individually to the child and placed above his sheet of paper. The child is told that he will copy seven designs that are to be presented one at a time. Specific directions may include such statements as: "Make one just like it on your paper" or "Make one like this" or "Copy this." The child should not be given directions as to location or organization. The forms can be presented individually or on a group basis.

Evaluation: Several methods of scoring are available. The Winter Haven Lions Research Foundation has a teachers' test manual that can be used to score the copy forms, as do Eugene B. Roach and Newell C. Kephart in their *The Purdue Perceptual-Motor Survey*. It is recommended here that each figure be individually scored on the 0-3–point scale:
   0. Unrecognizable drawing of figure
   1. Recognizable, but inadequate, drawing with poor execution of angulation, position, size, and neatness.
   2. Recognizable drawing, with only minor variations in regard to angulation, position, size, and neatness.
   3. Adequate figure that is positioned correctly, exhibits closure, correct angulation, position, size, and neatness.

Other types of copy-form tests, where children copy or reproduce figures from memory, are the *White-Phillips Visual Motor Test*, the *Visuo-Motor Designs* (*Lazarus Copy Forms*), the *Bender Visual-Motor Gestalt Test*, and the *Benton Visual Retention Test*.

OCULAR CONTROL

The relationship between visual inputs and motor patterns is one of the most important aspects of perceptual development. N. C. Kephart diagrams a model of the perceptual process, of which vision is one input.[3] In his discussion he states that neural impulses are transmitted to the sensory projection areas of the cerebral cortex where they are integrated into present and past experiences. Impulses are then sent to the motor area of the cortex, which generates muscle movements. Continual information is synthesized in terms of the accuracy of the movement taking place. This information is analogous to a feedback mechanism and allows for a high degree of accuracy of muscular activity. This theoretical explanation can account for the fine coordination between hand-eye movements, such as in writing or drawing.

The determination of ocular control can be evaluated by examining the

[2]*"Perceptual Ability and School Achievement,"* doctoral dissertation, Purdue University, Lafayette, Indiana, 1956. Available from Winter Haven Lions Club, Winter Haven, Florida.
[3]*The Slow Learner in the Classroom*, Columbus, Ohio, Charles E. Merrill Books, Inc., 1960.

performance of the child's eyes as they operate together, separately, and in convergence. The relevance of ocular development is that children need consistent, accurate information in order to perceive and synthesize. When there is faulty ocular control, the two eyes may not work together, with one lagging behind the other; the eyes may wander or lose their target; they may move in an uneven, uncoordinated fashion; or the head may move rather than the eyes. Convergence or the position of the two eyes in conjunction with the stimulus creates a triangular form. This triangle is longer at the apex as the distance between the eyes and the target increases, and shorter as the distance decreases. Control may be difficult to maintain as the target either moves closer to or further away from the child.

Ocular Pursuit

Equipment: Pencil or penlight and occluder.

Procedure: The examiner should sit on a chair facing the child, who is also seated.

A.   Both eyes. The examiner holds the pencil 20 inches from, and directly in front of, the child's eyes and slowly moves the pencil along in a circular motion. The radius of the circle should be about 20 inches. The child is asked to follow the pencil with his eyes and should be directed to move his eyes only. The examiner should move his pencil back and forth along the circumference of the circle, often breaking it up into quarters. He should then perform a vertical line, a horizontal line, and a diagonal line, as in an X shape.

Evaluation:

   0.   Child cannot move eyes without moving head; he loses target and cannot regain it.
   1.   Eye movements are uneven; child loses contact with target but can regain it; at midline discrepancy noted; contact maintained primarily with one eye.
   2.   Eye contact is maintained, but minor unevenness is apparent; one eye dominates while the other one wanders at "corners."
   3.   Contact maintained at all times without overshooting the target; eyes work together.

B.   Right eye only. The right eye is occluded, with a cover or an occluder, by the child. The examiner repeats the activities as noted in A. Evaluation is on the same 4-point scale.

C.   Left eye only. The left eye is occluded, with a cover or an occluder, by the child. The examiner repeats the activities as noted in A. Evaluation is on the same 4-point scale.

D.   Convergence. Here again the examiner is seated facing the child. He starts this procedure by having the pencil 18 inches in front of the child's eyes and slowly bringing it closer to the child's nose until there is a distance of 4 inches. The examiner should carefully observe the child's ability to focus continually as the pencil draws nearer. At that point the child is asked to look at the examiner's nose and then back again at the pencil. When the eyes break to focus on the far-point target, one eye may break faster than the other. As they refocus on the near-point target, there may be some searching or readjusting, and only one eye may be on target while the other eye is "turned off" and staring straight ahead or slightly to one side. Evaluation is on the same 4-point scale as in A.

SUMMARY

These initial aspects of perception are readily evaluated by the classroom teacher or by paraprofessionals. Scores may be summed up and divided by the number of evaluations achieved. This number gives the average or mean score. It can be used to give a general picture of a child's development. A more specific and practical use, however, is to use each score by itself and to compare the child's level of achievement from one area to another. Comparison of average or specific scores after the child has engaged in training activities allows the teacher or student to see the magnitude of change that has been achieved.[4]

The following areas of perception are not correlated, and the teacher must reach her own conclusion as to the level of development that the child has achieved.

AUDITORY PERCEPTION

The child's ability to locate and respond appropriately to sounds is of crucial importance in assisting his development and in making his school experience meaningful. His ability to listen and to attend to auditory cues and information perceived through this sense encompasses a large part of the kinds of information he receives throughout his waking hours. It is essential that the teacher be able to determine whether the child can respond to aural cues, whether the child is able to distinguish between similarities and differences in sounds, whether he can identify sounds, and whether he can distinguish between sequence and grading of sounds. Teachers can utilize many interesting games to determine the ability of children to attend to sounds and to assess the depth of their listening ability. For instance, a teacher may employ the "echo game," where she whispers a word to one child and in turn the child whispers to the next child and so on, until the last child is asked to repeat what he heard. Children are often asked to duplicate rhythms and a variety of sounds to help them appreciate the gradations and sequences of different sounds, as well as to help them learn to discriminate differences in the directions from which the sounds are emitted.

One standardized test that is used to evaluate auditory discrimination is the instrument designed by Joseph M. Wepman, the *Auditory Discrimination*

[4]Many of these evaluation items have been adopted from material in E. G. Roach and N. C. Kephart, *The Purdue Perceptual Motor Survey,* Columbus, Ohio, Charles E. Merrill, 1966. For further information the reader is referred to this publication.

Test, which has two forms. This test allows the examiner to evaluate the child and to come out with a score that is used to determine his degree of auditory discrimination. Copies of the test and directions for its use can be obtained by writing to Joseph M. Wepman, Ph.D., 950 East 59th Street, Chicago 37, Illinois.

LANGUAGE DEVELOPMENT

The child's ability to communicate verbally allows the teacher to appreciate not only how the child is able to describe his particular experiences, but also how he attempts to communicate these experiences and their meaningfulness to others. Opportunities for verbal communication in the classroom are essential to increasing communication skills between teacher and child and between the child and his peers. The ability to communicate successfully and distinctly helps the child to feel that he can relate to others, thereby increasing his own self-esteem. Children's verbal facility can be evaluated by listening to their spontaneous language in either a teacher-to-child or child-to-child interaction, by involving the children in group discussions, or through role playing. Specific instruments for evaluating children's language development are best seen in the *Illinois Test of Psycholinguistic Abilities*, by Samuel A. Kirk and James J. McCarthy. This test is given to children and is broken down into nine areas. The test individually measures several abilities, such as receptive and expressive language, association, and sequential memory. The test has several functions, and parts of it may be used for specific purposes.

CONCEPTUAL ABILITIES

The child's ability to use reasoning in understanding his world is of profound importance in developing his ability to deal effectively with the events he encounters. Children's conceptual abilities vary as a function of their age, and the necessary kinds of foundations must be laid so that the child can build upon these to enlarge his capacity for reasoning. His ability to organize his thinking comes, in large part, when he is able to classify and categorize stimuli into organized groups and subgroups that have coherent and cohesive meaning. There are often a variety of criteria to which children can respond in sorting stimuli or objects so that they fit into organized patterns. Such abilities also include the process of discrimination, noting similarities and differences between stimuli, and being able to generalize this information from one area to another. These processes lead to the development of concepts that, in turn, the child is able to transfer from one learning situation to another, thus extending the concepts he has internalized with more dimension and meaning.

One of the test instruments that best determines the child's vocabulary and conceptual abilities is the *Peabody Picture Vocabulary Test*. This test must be administered individually, and it gives quite quickly an accurate indication of the child's level of intellectual ability.

41

SUMMARY

In summary, a number of specific areas have been delineated that are useful in understanding the child's level of competence in many areas, and this understanding can be used to determine the particular kinds of curriculum that will be most useful in terms of making his school experiences meaningful. Of course, there are numerous other areas of significance that can be explored, such as the child's social-emotional adjustment and development. However, it is felt that the areas listed here are the most crucial in assisting the classroom teacher in formulating a systematic program whereby the child's total development may be assessed.

TRAINING PROGRAMS

Levels of perceptual development not only can be recognized, but they can be modified and changed through appropriate and systematic structuring of curriculum within the school programs. This training should be introduced for specific reasons. One method is to use perceptually geared activities in the lower elementary grades and kindergarten as a way of promoting increased perceptual abilities and skills. Such a program would have its ameliorative effects, as well as tending to minimize or decrease existing deficiencies. These activities would increase "readiness skills," which are so necessary for a successful involvement with academic materials. Another method is to work with small groups of children for a short period each day as is done with reading groups. The teachers should be trained by personnel who are knowledgeable in the area of sensory-perceptual development and its applications to the classroom. The classroom teacher, physical education teacher, teachers' assistants, teachers' aides, or paraprofessionals can be utilized to work with classes or groups of children to maximize their perceptual development so that their encounter with academic material will not be hindered or wasted. Such programs will maximize the child's total development and growth in school and will thereby enhance his opportunity for success in academic situations.

Although specific activities will be spelled out, it is important for the teacher to recognize that no specific activity is a goal in and of itself. The idea of activities is to allow the child experience in crucial dimensions so that he can generalize the skills that he learns to new and varied activities in his life. For instance, the child's awareness of auditory discrimination is not an end in itself but is essential in his ability to understand and communicate with others. Similarly, his knowledge of hopping on one foot at a time can be generalized to a variety of new motor skills, and he should be given opportunities to express himself creatively through his hopping. For example, he can be asked to hop as many different ways as he can think of. A further extension of this is for the child to incorporate these new hopping activities into his regular movements as he goes from one place to another, or to try as many different ways as possible of crossing from one point to another.

Much of the equipment used by the teacher for the initial evaluation can be incorporated in the training activities. It is essential that any curriculum incorporate activities in the gross motor area to ensure that adequate foundations and skills have been developed so that the child can use these skills to elaborate and to modify more refined and detailed skills. Listed below are suggested activities for children that will enhance and further these areas of development:

GROSS MOTOR MOVEMENTS

1. Walking board

It is possible to use the same walking board as was used to evaluate the children. The procedure is to have the children walk on the board without their shoes. The child should be positioned by the teacher, standing erect and with his eyes focused on an object that is at eye level at the end of the board. The teacher should continually emphasize that it is important for the child to walk slowly, and she should encourage him to get the "feel" of the board with his feet and to imagine as vividly as he can what the board feels like. Such concentration encourages increased feedback from the various sensory areas of the body, which gives information to the child for use in a number of activities. In walking forward, the child should first be encouraged to keep his hands at his sides or to use them for balance, and later to keep his arms out straight, away from the body. After he has some experience in walking back and forth across the board, he can reverse his direction and walk backwards. Again, he should be looking straight ahead with his eyes focused on the spot, which is at eye level. He can also walk on the board sideways. For this procedure he stands sideways with his feet together and then moves one foot, puts his weight on it, and then moves his other foot to join the first. This is one way in which he can walk sideways. He can also cross one foot in front of another and, finally, one foot in back of another. At all times he should be encouraged to walk slowly and to maintain his balance.

When the children can successfully complete these tasks, it is encouraging for them to attempt new maneuvers on the walking board. Other variations include turning on the board, bouncing on the board, or taking a certain amount of steps forwards, backwards, or sideways. Here, the child has to concentrate on maintaining his balance and keeping a correct posture, while at the same time concentrating on the number of steps he must make. Some children have difficulty in walking on the board, as the distance between the board and the ground varies. This height variation is accomplished by placing large blocks under both ends of the board. This revised spatial orientation involves a new dimension that the child must learn. As a further elaboration, he can walk on the board on its narrow edge. To do this, secure the board so that it cannot tip or fall on its side. Of course, many other variations and elaborations are possible, and there need not be any limitations as to the variety of activities attempted.

The usefulness of the walking board is that it teaches balance and laterality, which are skills that can be generalized by the child to new situations. The child can be encouraged to say "Left" and "Right" as he walks across the board, to count each time he moves his foot, or to repeat letters of the alphabet with each movement. Children who have difficulty in maintaining their balance on the board may practice these activities by walking across the floor on a strip of paper that has approximately the same dimensions as that of the board.

2. Jumping, hopping, skipping, and balance

A number of activities can be taken from the evaluation task and incorporated in the training program. For instance, the child can jump in a variety of ways that are appropriate to his level of development. He can jump with two feet together or on one foot at a time. The feet can then be alternated. He can be encouraged to take small jumps, large jumps, jumps to the left, jumps to the right, and jumps behind.

The child may need to hold on to an object at waist height in order to hop, if he does not have adequate balance and control. This assistance may be necessary for younger children. The child is asked to hop once on the right foot a number of times. He can then hop once on the left and once on the right, until he can maintain this activity in a rhythmic, controlled manner. He can also hop twice on the right foot and twice on the left, maintaining this activity with smooth alternation from one side to another. On a more complicated level, he can learn to hop twice on the left foot and once on the right, or vice versa.

Skipping is a more complicated activity, as it involves the shifting of weight from one side to the other, as well as the use of a small hop—all done in a continuous, coordinated fashion. Children who do not learn how to skip should first be encouraged to learn how to hop and to alternate from one side to the other until they can do this successfully.

Balance exercises are varied and involve the possibility of using many activities. For instance, a child can be instructed to stand for ten seconds while holding one leg and one arm out to the side. He can then alternate sides. He can stand on tiptoes for ten seconds, or he can swing one foot back and forth as he is standing on the other.

The balance board is a worthwhile piece of equipment in increasing the child's sense of balance. This is a board that is approximately 16 inches square with various sized "posts" underneath, attached by a nut and bolt so that they can be interchanged. The size of the posts can be 3, 4, or 5 inches square. The children place themselves on the balance board with their feet at the sides, and they learn to rock back and forth, from side to side, or forwards and backwards. They can also be encouraged to touch various corners of the balance board, such as the front left corner or the rear right corner. The child should hold his hands out for balance and attempt to focus his eyes on a spot at eye level on the wall. Various exercises at the chalkboard can be done while the child maintains his balance on the balance board.

44

3. Identification of body parts and their location

The simplest way of teaching the identification of body parts is by having the child actually touch various parts of his body and experience for himself the sensations that he gets from such activities. An easy classroom activity that reinforces this experience is the "Simon Says" game. The teacher asks the children to touch their hands, touch their shoulders, etc., until a variety of parts have been named and touched. In another variation, the teacher stands in front of the room and asks the children to imitate his movements. He should vary the positions of his arms in terms of horizontal, vertical, and other angulations, with the idea that the children will copy these movements and experience for themselves the feelings they encounter when their arms and hands are in various positions.

Another activity that helps children to appreciate the parts of their body and the left-right dimension is called "Angels in the Snow." Here, the children are asked to lie on their backs with their feet together and their hands at their sides. Their shoes are removed and their fingers are touching the floor. They first respond in a unilateral way—one side of the body operating at a time. For instance, the teacher will say "Left" to the children, and the children will extend their left hands to the side, while turning their heads (from looking at the ceiling) to the left side where they can observe their fingers. At the same time, the left leg is extended along the floor as far as possible. The teacher then responds with "Down," or a similar command This is followed with the command, "Right," whereupon the children use the same movements as before, turning their heads to the right, extending their right hands to shoulder height, and extending their right legs.

Children who cannot follow through with these simultaneous movements can successfully accomplish more simple movements by moving one arm or leg at a time. When they are able to accomplish this satisfactorily, the arm and leg movements can be integrated along with the head movements. After a unilateral movement is achieved in a coordinated fashion, the child can learn to operate bilaterally, using both sides of his body together. For instance, when the teacher says "Left," the child moves his left hand and turns his head to the left, while extending the right leg; conversely, when he says "Right," the student turns his head to the right as he extends his right arm and left leg to the side. These exercises should be done in both a supine and prone position—that is, when the child is on his back and when he is on his stomach.

FORM PERCEPTION

The child's ability to develop directionality and hand-eye coordination and to recognize the various dimensions inherent in particular characteristics of stimuli are some of the necessary ingredients in accurate form perception. After he has been evaluated in terms of his level of development, several training activities are useful in increasing his skills in this area.

One of the best methods is to use templates of various geometric figures cut out of cardboard or fiberboard. Characteristic geometric figures are, again, the circle, square, triangle, rectangle, and horizontal and vertical diamond. These figures should be approximately 6 inches in width or height and of sturdy enough material so that the children can use them daily without destroying the contours of each figure. The children are asked to put these templates at eye level on a chalkboard with masking tape and to trace the outlines of each of the figures with their forefingers until they feel familiar with the particular form and characteristics of each shape. Once the children have had practice in touching and guiding their fingers around the contours of each shape, they may use chalk to draw the particular shapes, taking ten or twenty trips around the contours of each. Children can also do these activities with their nonwriting or nondominant hand as a way of getting information from another source regarding the characteristics of various stimuli. They can trace the contours of the figures in the air by moving their arms or fingers in the various shapes of the objects. When they show proficiency in staying on the line of the templates, more difficulties can be instituted, such as having them draw around the actual geometric figures themselves, rather than tracing the outlines of figures that have been cut out. The child can vary his activity by drawing with heavy chalk, regular-sized chalk, or colored chalk. He can do similar activities with various sizes of geometric shapes, rather than the ones he used originally.

While the child is gaining experience working with geometric shapes, he can also use various other chalkboard activities that will help him to free his motor movements and build up a repertoire of movements, habits, and patterns that will be useful to him in later academic work. Initially, he should be free to scribble on the chalkboard and make whatever random movements he might enjoy. He should then stand in front of the chalkboard with his eyes focused on an X at eye level and draw a circle with his preferred hand. After he has made a large circle, approximately 20 inches in diameter, the direction of the circle is noted, and he is asked to draw a circle in the opposite direction. With his nonpreferred hand, he should attempt to make a circle approximately 20 inches in diameter, after which he can be asked to reverse the direction. When children are able to make these circles and maintain some degree of accuracy in terms of the circularity and positioning of the lines, they can make two circles at a time, using both hands. They can make circles with both hands going in a clockwise position or in a counterclockwise position. Further elaboration is introduced when the hands go in opposite directions. At a later time, the directions are reversed, so that the children enjoy a number of directions in terms of both preferred and nonpreferred hand movements. Similar types of activities can be instituted with other geometric figures, such as the square, diamond, rectangle, and triangle.

Games that are often exciting involve making an X on the blackboard in front of the child's eyes, and then having him draw a line from the X in front of him to the one on his left or right. This can be further developed by having two X's, one on his left and one on his right, at various degrees on the blackboard. Here, he has to make movements that extend from one side of

46

his body to the other, crossing the midline of his body. An innovation of the game is where the teacher makes an X and the child has to draw a straight line from that X to another X. This continues, with the teacher drawing random X's and the child being asked to continue to draw straight lines. These lines may intersect each other, at which point the child must be able to ignore or not react to the previously drawn lines or X's, thereby giving him further training in figure-ground relationships.

With his eyes closed, the child can be given templates of various geometric shapes and be asked to tell what they are. He can also match various kinds of tactile stimuli, using materials such as wood, plastic, paper, or textiles. He might be asked to match those that feel alike or to grade them from coarse to fine. Various kinds of stimuli can be graduated in terms of coarseness or fineness of the material and can be discriminated not only through the tactile sense of the child's fingers, but also by using his nose, his tongue, his elbow, or his feet. These kinds of stimulations offer the child additional dimensions by which to observe differing characteristics of stimuli.

Form perception is further developed by offering the child opportunities to work with materials such as puzzles, where he must learn to react to both shapes of contour and color to guide him in placing particular pieces. Puzzles can be made more difficult by keeping the color constant so that the contour of the individual pieces is the only dimension that varies. The use of pegboards is an additional aid in assisting growth in form perception. Here, the child can construct his own figures on a pegboard, or he can learn to copy increasingly complex designs where they intersect with one another. Children can also learn to construct designs from memory, where the model is no longer available to them. This aids in visual memory and is useful with academic tasks.

OCULAR CONTROL

The ability of the child to focus his eyes continually upon necessary stimuli, either on the blackboard or when presented with desk work, is essential for progress in school. After the child has been diagnosed in terms of his level of ocular-control development, various tasks and activities are available for enhancing his ability. For instance, one simple game that is fun for children and that enhances ocular control and hand-eye coordination is the flashlight game. Here, the teacher has a large flashlight, and the child has a small flashlight. The teacher moves his flashlight beam around the room, and the child is instructed to keep his light within the beam of the teacher's light as he makes various movements. With his flashlight, the teacher can trace geometric shapes that have been drawn on the blackboard, or he can make various of these geometric shapes on the wall, and the children can follow.

Another excellent activity is to mount a small ball on the end of a string and instruct the child to keep his eyes focused on the ball at all times, without moving his head, as the ball swings back and forth or in various directions. Other children can assist in this activity so that the class can be broken down into groups or pairs of children. The children can then take turns with this activity. Another technique, using the swinging ball, is for the child to use a long round stick with two stripes as it swings in order to maintain its swinging motion. The object of the game is to attempt to get the child to hit the ball with increasing accuracy with one or another of the two stripes. These activities can be further complicated by occluding, or covering, one eye. The child can attempt to touch the ball with the stick by using first one hand and then the other hand to further increase coordination.

Visual memory is a necessary concomitant of vision training and allows the child to remember and to reproduce stimuli that he has received. Exercises can be made into games. For instance, several children can line up and walk behind a screen, and then one child will be missing as they walk out the other side. The class will be asked who is missing and on what end of the screen he was last seen. Another game is "store," where the children are allowed to view a number of articles. The articles are then covered and several articles removed. The children are asked which articles are no longer present. Of course, the converse can be done, where more articles are added and the child is asked to pick out the additional pieces. This game can also be played on the chalkboard. A particular shape is drawn and part of it is erased. The child is then asked to put in the missing part. Another activity is to show the children pictures. After they have viewed them, they are asked to name as many details as they can. Flashcard games, where the child can view an object for only a second or so, assist in developing visual memory. Visual recall can also be elaborated by delaying the child's responses. Here, the child has to wait a certain number of seconds before he can respond with the correct details or answers. A useful instrument for developing visual memory is the tachistoscope, which varies the speed of stimuli that are projected on a screen. The children are asked to reproduce or state what they viewed.[5]

AUDITORY PERCEPTION

The child's ability to respond to auditory cues is a necessary condition for success in the classroom situation. He needs to know how to respond to auditory cues as a way of developing impulse control and to focus upon directions given by the teacher. Activities that enhance this ability should be instituted within the classroom at the beginning of the year, and once they have become a pattern, they can be maintained without difficulty. These procedures allow the teacher, without duress or emotionality on his part, to get the child's attention immediately. For example, the children are told to "freeze" when they hear a certain signal. They are encouraged to engage in this activity a number of times until they can do it successfully. Activities that focus on gradations in sounds can be done by using the entire class or small groups.

[5] Many of the activities described here have been adopted from material found in N. C. Kephart, *The Slow Learner in the Classroom* Columbus, Ohio, Charles E. Merrill, 1960. The reader is referred to this volume as well as the more recent publications, C. M. Chaney and N. C. Kephart, *Motoric Aids to Perceptual Training* Columbus, Ohio, Charles E. Merrill, 1968 and M. L. Ebersole, N. C. Kephart, and J. Ebersole, *Steps to Achievement in the Slow Learner* Columbus, Ohio, Charles E. Merrill, 1968.

For instance, the teacher can introduce various kinds of sounds, such as a musical instrument, an animal noise, a tapping of the foot or finger, etc., and the children are asked to identify the sounds. The task becomes more difficult when it is done behind a screen so that the children cannot see what is making the sound. Children can be encouraged to make certain sounds, and other children are instructed to guess what they are doing. The teacher can use a series of sounds that are graded, and the child is instructed to determine which sound is the loudest, the softest, and the various gradations in between. Auditory memory is illustrated by using a sequence of sounds. The child listens to the teacher make a series of sounds and then attempts to duplicate these sounds himself.

LANGUAGE DEVELOPMENT

The child's ability to communicate verbally is one of the most important skills. Group discussions led by the teacher are often an informal way of encouraging participation in setting up their own telephone conversations or in acting out TV programs. Children can be asked to describe verbally a picture and the details they see in it or to make up a story about a picture. Various kinds of role playing help the child to appreciate the kinds of communication that take place between groups of people, such as between parents and children or between teachers and children. Puppets can be used to assist children in interacting with one another. Numerous other kinds of verbal activities and verbal games that will facilitate communication between pupil and teacher are available and can be readily thought of by the teacher.

CONCEPTUAL ABILITIES

The child's intellectual or conceptual faculties can be tremendously enhanced by the proper sequence of experiences and stimuli in his life. A careful appreciation of the development of children can be used by the teacher to facilitate growth within the child. The child who has perceptual deficits and an inability to communicate verbally cannot use whatever innate conceptual abilities he might possess. Therefore, it is seen that these things work hand in hand with each other and for each other, and for the most adequate development of the child, it is essential that all of these areas be coordinated in a meaningful fashion. Various theoretical notions regarding children's cognitive development have been discussed by Jean Piaget and Jerome Bruner. These two theorists offer many worthwhile explanations of children's intellectual development, and their framework can be used by the classroom teacher to modify her curriculum so that the child's intellectual development is fully stimulated and enhanced.

The child can be presented with a variety of objects that vary in only one dimension, such as shape. For instance, he can have a variety of circles that range from large to small, and he is requested to put them in ascending or descending order of largeness. He can also be asked to sort a variety of stimuli of different shapes, such as circles, squares, triangles, diamonds, etc. These shapes can have two dimensions, such as color and shape. Increasingly complex tasks involve stimuli that the child has to sort out into those groups that seem to go together. For instance, he can be presented with a number of miniature toys, such as cars, trucks and motorcycles; with animals, such as horses, cows, sheep, dogs; with people, such as fathers, mothers, teachers, policemen; with structures, such as houses and barns; etc. He is asked to sort out all of these things once they have been put into a large pile. He is then asked to state the reasons for the kinds of sortings he has made. Children also have to understand such concepts as opposites and similarities. To accomplish this they can be given examples such as "Fire is *hot*, but ice is *cold*"; similarities can be explored by such examples as "Candy and sugar are both *sweet*." Concepts that involve the child's ability to describe his relationship to objects can be explored by having him put his foot *in* the circle, to step *out* of a box, to walk *around* a table, to crawl *under* a chair, etc. Various kinds of adverbs, such as to jump *slowly, quickly, sadly,* etc., are useful in terms of helping a child increase the ways in which he can describe a particular characteristic of an object. Riddles are also useful and excite the child's curiosity and enthusiasm. For instance, "What is black and flat, and we write on it? What is it?" The teacher can use his own ingenuity in creating various other kinds of tasks with conceptual bases that are pertinent to his students' needs.

FIVE: EXTENDING PRESCHOOL PROGRAMS

In discussing the preschool and kindergarten programs, let us first note that we are not attempting to provide a total curriculum in one chapter, since this is obviously an impossible task. What will be attempted is an indication of some guiding propositions and a description of some aspects of the program that follow from these propositions and that would probably not be present in a standard or typical preschool or kindergarten. By emphasizing what would be different about early-childhood programs for inner-city children, we hope to give the reader some ideas about beneficial innovations in programs that already exist. If one has no experience with preschool and kindergarten programs and is starting to build a program "from scratch," then other sources should be consulted in addition to this one.

It may be that preschool programs will be new to many schools, but the trend is toward increasing such programs. Government subsidizing of Headstart programs has undoubtedly speeded acceptance of the preschool program as a vital, contributing factor in the education of inner-city children. It has also provided a "laboratory" for the study and comparison of various alternative programs. Unfortunately, not all of the programs have been as successful as we might hope, and not all of the research has been as definitive as we would like. However, some things of value have been learned.

Studies that have attempted to assess growth in IQ as a result of preschool training have had somewhat ambiguous results, though they tend to indicate that any gains shown during the preschool years are gradually lost after entrance into kindergarten.[1] A study by R. Formanek, which focused on behavioral observations of children in a Headstart program, has provided some findings that are more meaningful for our purposes.[2] This study compared children's behavior in free-play settings with their behavior in teacher-directed settings. Independent, productive behavior and sociable behavior were greater in free-play settings. Passive, conformist behavior and restless, distractible behavior and daydreaming were greater in teacher-directed settings.

When the children were followed up in kindergarten, it was found that behavior in the teacher-directed settings had changed. Independent, productive behavior, which had increased in the summer Headstart program, had declined in the kindergarten program. Passive, uninvolved behavior, fidgeting and daydreaming, which had decreased during the summer Headstart program, increased considerably in the kindergarten program. It was noted that the amount of time children spent in teacher-directed settings had also increased considerably.

There was, as might be expected, considerable variation in the behavior patterns of individual children. At the end of the Headstart program, two groups of children were identified on the basis of their variability scores. Those children whose behavior changed most from one setting to another, but whose behavior remained appropriate to the setting, were the *high-variability* group. Those children whose behavior showed the least amount of change from one setting to another were the *low-variability* group. It was predicted that the high-variability group would be successful in later school achievement, while the low-variability group would be unsuccessful. This prediction was confirmed with a high degree of accuracy the following year, when almost all of the low-variability children were retained in kindergarten and all of the high-variability children entered first grade.

The results of the Formanek study would seem to suggest that children's ability to adapt their behavior to varied settings is a crucial factor in their

[1] C. Bereiter and S. Engelmann, *Teaching Disadvantaged Children in the Preschool*, Englewood Cliffs, New Jersey, Prentice-Hall, Inc., 1966.
[2] "Headstart Follow-Up, 1965-1968: Validation of an Observational Instrument for Predictions Regarding School Success," paper presented to the American Educational Research Association, Los Angeles, February, 1969.

52

school achievement. Put another way, those children who learn to play the student role most quickly are the ones most likely to succeed as students. The results further suggest that desirable behavior patterns are developed more readily when free-play settings account for a substantial proportion of the school day. This is not to be interpreted to mean that teacher-directed settings should be eliminated entirely. If there were no variety of settings, then children would have no opportunity to learn to adapt their behavior to changes in setting.

These implications, when considered in light of the work on behavior modification previously discussed, lead to our first guidelines for a preschool and kindergarten program. These are as follows:

One, the primary function of the preschool and kindergarten program should be to help children learn the roles appropriate to various school settings.

Two, behavior-modification techniques should be utilized to help children learn these roles in a manner that is conducive to development of positive self-concepts.

Three, an attempt should be made to give children extensive experience in each of three different settings: free play, teacher-directed group work, and teacher-directed individual work. These are the major kinds of settings to be utilized in the first- and second-grade curriculum, as outlined in Chapter 3. Free play will correspond to independent investigation, which will be an important part of the uncommon learning centers. Teacher-directed group work will correspond to the later work in reading and mathematics groups. Teacher-directed individual work will correspond to the individual study periods for reading and mathematics in the first and second grades.

In this way, children will learn to play the various student roles expected of them in the early grades. However, this is not the only job to be accomplished in a preschool or kindergarten program. Children will also need to learn some "content" that will help them in the later grades.

FORMAL LESSONS IN THE PRESCHOOL PROGRAM

There is some disagreement among early-childhood specialists as to what form this learning of content should take. Some, such as C. Bereiter, urge the use of formal lessons. Other, more traditional, educators insist that informal learning is best at this age and that children suffer emotionally if they are given "too much structure." It is interesting to note, however, that this latter group generally adhere to rather rigid time schedules for various kinds of activities (e.g., 9 to 9:30 A.M., free play; 9:30 to 10, "circle" activities; 10 to 10:20, snack, etc.). This practice is defended on the grounds that it gives children security to know what is going to happen next. The fact that this is also imposing a definite "structure" on children seems to be ignored.

It may well be that the whole argument about whether a preschool or kindergarten program contains "too much structure" or "too little structure" is based on a false distinction. We submit that there are many different types of structure. No environment is really unstructured. The first question to be answered is what *type* of structure is most advantageous for young children from the inner city? In attempting to answer this question, we should like to review another interesting study.

An investigation by S. Greenberg and R. Formanek into young children's understanding of relational terms such as *up* and *down* indicated definite differences among groups attending different types of preschool programs.[3] Two groups of children were from middle-class homes and were attending private nursery schools. Two groups of children were from "disadvantaged" homes and were attending Headstart programs. One of the private schools and one of the Headstart programs ran rather traditional nursery school programs, with an emphasis on free play and art activities. The other two schools attempted to teach concepts through the use of more teacher-directed lessons.

Children's understanding of relational terms was tested by action (it was determined whether they could go *under the table, behind the table*, etc.) and by representation (they were asked to identify pictures that showed the ball *under the table*, etc.). Middle-class children who had had more teacher-directed lessons scored highest in their understanding of various terms. Disadvantaged children who had had more teacher-directed lessons scored about the same as middle-class children in a university-sponsored program of the traditional type. Apparently the emphasis on directed concept learning did have an effect on children's awareness of relational terms, although the terms, as such, had not been taught in these lessons.

THE MEANING OF "STRUCTURE"

With these results in mind, let us return to our discussion of types of "structure." One important way to structure the child's environment is through the selection and organization of the objects that surround him. At home these objects would include furniture and toys; at school they would include furniture and teaching materials. The nursery school that has children put blocks away in different bins, according to their length, is probably teaching the child to be aware of length as one property that objects have. The nursery school that has black dolls as well as white has a greater chance of teaching the child that babies of both colors are beautiful. Thus, the way in which the concrete objects in the environment are selected and arranged structures what the child perceives and what attitudes he will have. This type of structure exists even in so-called informal settings.

Another way to structure the child's environment is by selecting and scheduling his general activity. At home this could take the form of the following

---

[3] "The Preschooler's Relational Concepts as Tested in Object and Representational Form," paper presented to the American Educational Research Association, Los Angeles, February, 1969.

kinds of comments from mother: "Your breakfast's ready"; "It's time to watch Captain Kangaroo on TV"; "Why don't you go outside and play with your friends"; "I'll read you a story before bedtime." At school it may take the form, noted earlier, of assigning a particular time block for each kind of activity. The child who is constantly told, "No, you can't give your baby a bath, because you'll get all wet," or, "Turn off those cartoons on TV now; it's time to eat your lunch," learns that the problem he is interested in pursuing is less important than obeying or complying with orders. The child who moves from one activity to another on his own is learning to evaluate alternatives and make decisions. Thus, the scheduling of activities in the child's environment also structures his learning of skills and attitudes.

A third type of structure involves the selection and organization of specific operations or procedures that the child uses with various materials. At home this could take the form of teaching a child how to play a simple card game, then later, telling him that he should not use the cards to make a road for his trucks. At school it might take the form of demonstrating how to use a pair of scissors and directing the children to cut out shapes that have been drawn on the paper for them. The child who is never given any suggestions about how to use a crayon will probably not become very adept at coloring. The child who is taught to use only the point of the crayon and to "stay inside the lines" will give up attempts to explore or imagine other uses. Thus, the selection and organization of procedures to be used with various materials structures the skills and attitudes that the child learns.

A fourth type of structure involves the selection of people with whom the child will interact. At home this may take the form of sending a neighbor's child home when an argument starts or of taking the child to the home of a friend so that the children can play together. At school this may take the form of grouping children by age or ability. Since children learn through social interaction, the selection of people with whom the child will interact also structures what kind of information he gathers and what kind of social prejudices he develops.

There are other types of structure that may occur in the child's environment. For example, the environment of sound at home may be structured to include popular or classical music, or perhaps, no music at all. The environment of sound at school may be structured to allow complete bedlam or to maintain complete silence. Our goal here is not to identify every possible type of structure but, rather, to point out that many types of structure do exist, while an "unstructured" setting does *not* exist in the real world.

There are many other aspects of the notion of "structure" to explore in addition to the various types of structure, and the other aspects also have definite consequences for the educational process. As we have pointed out, structure exists in every situation. That structure may be consciously provided with a particular goal in mind, as when a special class of mentally retarded children is formed in order to give these children a curriculum adapted to their particular needs. On the other hand, the structure may be unconsciously provided with no awareness of the consequences, as when a teacher has students' desks placed in rows because that was where they were when she first entered the classroom.

The various structures that exist in any classroom setting have educational consequences, whether or not they are consciously provided; but the school can only be said to control the educational process to the extent that it consciously plans to provide the particular structures that will enhance its educational goals.

This brings us to another aspect of structure. A structure that is consciously provided may be determined on the basis of two different kinds of goals. Some structures are consciously provided with particular learning goals in mind. Other structures are consciously provided with economy or efficiency as the major goal. Examples of the latter kind of decision are: grouping children "homogeneously" so that the teacher can plan lessons for the entire class rather than worrying about individual differences; seating children alphabetically so that attendance can be taken easily; instituting a "no-talking" rule in the cafeteria so that less adult supervision is needed. We might distinguish between these two types of consciously provided structures by labeling those based on learning goals *curriculum structures* and those based on efficiency goals *management structures*.

Another aspect of structure is its range or variance. Any given type of structure may vary along a continuum. For example, the selection and organization of objects might vary from almost random arrangements, where any object is simply dropped when one is finished with it, to neat-as-a-pin arrangements, with "a place for everything and everything in its place." The scheduling of activities can also vary widely, from the setting where a child does what he wants when he wants, even to eating when he feels like it rather than at specified mealtimes, to the setting where every minute is organized by mother. The selection and organization of specific procedures or operations to be used with various materials may range from an almost total lack of direction to giving the child precise specifications as to how any given material is to be used. The selection of children with whom the child will interact may vary from permitting the child to play with any and all comers, taking his "lumps" as best he may, to instructing the child to stay away from all children who are bigger than he, or who use "bad words," or who are black.

We should like to call this continuum, exhibited by the various types of structures, an *adaptation continuum*. We introduce this term because we find it useful to view the continuum in terms of the child's method of adapting to the structures that confront him at various points along the continuum. At one end of the continuum, where organization of the environment approaches randomness, the child must provide his own organization, using his own internal structures. At this point, his method of adaptation is primarily *assimilation*, in the Piagetian meaning of the term; that is, he uses the concepts already at his command to direct his perception and use of the environment.

At the other end of the continuum, where the environment is already highly organized, the child must subordinate his internal structures to the

56

organization that exists in reality. At this point, his method of adaptation is primarily *accommodation*.

In between these two points there is a middle ground. Here, there is some moderate organization of the environment. Here, the child must adjust somewhat to the organization that exists, but he must also bring his internal structures to bear in order to further organize and utilize the environment. Here, his method of adaptation is what Piaget calls *intellectual adaptation* or *equilibration*. This is the point on the continuum that permits the most growth or learning to occur.

VARYING STRUCTURE FOR THE INNER-CITY CHILD

The question that has frequently been asked about nursery school programs is: "Is it a structured program or an unstructured program?" If we consider the four aspects of structure outlined above, then this becomes a meaningless question. Rather, for any given situation or setting we need to ask the following four questions:

1. What types of structure are important in this setting?
2. Were these structures provided consciously or unconsciously?
3. If the structures were provided consciously, are they curriculum structures or management structures?
4. At what point on the adaptation continuum does each type of structure fall?

After this kind of analysis has been made, we can ask the crucial question:

5. What are the educational consequences of the combination of structures that exist in this particular setting?

As an example of where this kind of questioning leads us, let us take a free-play setting in a Headstart program. First of all, we note that there has been selection and organization of objects and that this has been consciously planned with a learning goal in mind; thus a curriculum structure exists. In this particular setting, this type of structure probably falls at a point somewhere between the midpoint and the assimilation end of the adaptation continuum, since the child is free to select the objects with which he will interact, within the range of possible objects provided.

Next we note that selection and scheduling of activities is present. Free play occurs at a particular time in the day, and not all activities are allowed even at this time in most schools. For instance, a teacher will probably not read a story to an individual child if the child requests it at this time. This type of structure has been consciously planned, partially with a learning goal in mind of letting the child explore on his own, partially with efficiency in mind in that activities that might get "messy" and require more adult supervision are generally not allowed. We might say, then, that a curriculum-management structure exists. This type of structure in a free-play setting probably falls somewhere between the midpoint and the assimilation end of the adaptation continuum, in that the child has free choice within a limited range.

57

A third type of structure that exists in this setting is the selection and organization of operations or procedures to be used with the materials. This is probably not consciously planned by the teacher. It would fall near the assimilation end of the adaptation continuum, since the child is generally free to use the materials as he chooses.

Finally, selection of people with whom the child interacts exists in this setting. There has been conscious planning in relation to the people who are available for interaction; they are children of a specific age and socioeconomic background and adults who are trained to work with them. This planning has been done with a learning goal in mind—that of providing special types of experiences needed by these particular children—so a curriculum structure exists. This structure would also fall between the midpoint and the assimilation end on the adaptation continuum, since the child has free choice within a limited range of possibilities. This analysis can be diagramed as follows:

SETTING: FREE PLAY, HEADSTART PROGRAM

Type of structure	Planning	Goal	Point on adaptation continuum
Selection and organization of objects	Conscious	Curriculum	Between midpoint and assimilation end
Selection and scheduling of activities	Conscious	Curriculum-management	Between midpoint and assimilation end
Selection and organization of operations and procedures	Unconscious		Near assimilation end
Selection of people with whom child interacts	Conscious	Curriculum	Between midpoint and assimilation end

The important question to consider on the basis of this analysis is: *What are the educational consequences of this combination of structures for these particular children?* If we believe the research on the disadvantaged child, then we must assume that the home background has provided the child with settings that are consistently structured so that they fall near the assimilation end of the adaptation continuum. The child is accustomed to making his own decisions about what things to use, what to do with them, when to do it, and with whom to do it. The major difference between this setting and his home environment is that there are more objects from which to choose. What the child is learning, then, is something about how the new objects can be handled. In his exploration of the new objects, however, he is rather dependent upon his own internal structures; that is, he will tend to try doing the same kinds of things with the new objects that he has previously learned to do with familiar objects. The variety of experiences he has previously had with objects is probably limited. Therefore, the learning that will occur in this setting for the inner-city child is rather limited.

The same setting may provide important learnings for the middle-class child of preschool age, whose home environment probably tends to provide settings that are consistently structured to fall nearer the accommodation end of the continuum. This child is getting important experience in making his own decisions when he is placed in the typical free-play setting. His exploration of new objects will have variety to it because he has already learned many ways of interacting with many different kinds of objects.

The free-play setting can be modified for the inner-city child to produce significant learnings, however. There are two ways in which such modification might occur. If the goal is to have the child learn new ways of operating with objects, then that type of structure can be altered within the free-play setting. Planning by the teacher would become conscious, and the goal would be curricular. This structure would move to a point between the midpoint and the accommodation end of the adaptation continuum. What this would mean in terms of teacher behavior is that after the child had selected an object and begun to play with it or explore it, the teacher would suggest a specific procedure to be used with the object and would demonstrate the procedure to the child. The suggestion should be couched in terms such as, "Here is something you can try," rather than, "This is what you're supposed to do with this."

Another way of modifying the free-play setting would be to change the structure of selecting people with whom the children will interact. Conscious planning here might include the curriculum goal of encouraging children to interact verbally with adults. This structure would then move to a point between the midpoint and the accommodation end of the adaptation continuum. In terms of teacher behavior, this would mean that the teacher would sit near the child as he plays and would talk with the child, describing the actions the child is performing, or asking the child to describe them.

This kind of modification of the setting puts the child in the position of accommodating to some aspect of the environment without forcing him to accommodate to several things at once. Thus, the child who has been accustomed to moving about with relative freedom does not experience frustration, but he does have an opportunity to learn.

Let us now turn to a setting of teacher-directed group work and consider the combinations of structures that might exist there. A typical example of such a setting in a preschool program is the reading of a story to a circle of children. The object (book) has been selected by the teacher, the operations (questions to be considered and answered) have been selected by the teacher, and the person with whom the child is to interact (listen to the teacher and answer the teacher's questions) has been selected by the teacher. The setting would be diagramed as follows:

Type of structure	Planning	Goal	Point on adaptation continuum
Selection and organization of objects	Conscious	Curriculum (learning to enjoy books)	Toward accommodation end
Selection and scheduling of activities	Conscious	Curriculum (learning to look and listen)	Toward accommodation end
Selection and organization of operations and procedures	Conscious	Curriculum (learning to be aware of sequence, interpret pictures, etc.)	Toward accommodation end
Selection of people with whom child interacts	Conscious	Management (maintaining relative quiet)	Toward accommodation end

In this type of setting there is too much accommodation required of an inner-city child, who is presumably accustomed to much freedom of movement. The educational consequence of this combination of structures is, therefore, that the child fails to learn what the teacher desires, because he is unable to make so many adjustments simultaneously. He probably does learn to dislike books and listening. To be of educational value to the inner-city child, this setting also needs some modification.

Two types of structure can be changed to modify this setting. The selection of the book can be made by the group of children, from among a number of books provided by the teacher. This moves the selection of objects to a point between the midpoint and the assimilation end of the adaptation continuum. In addition, the questions can be asked by the children rather than the teacher. This moves the selection of operations to a point near the assimilation end of the adaptation continuum, and while the planning of this structure is still conscious, the teacher's goal becomes to encourage the child to inquire about or explore the story.

These modifications change the educational consequences of the combination of structures so that a learning situation now exists. The child has control over some aspects of the environment and is able to handle the smaller amount of accommodation that is now required.

Finally, we might consider a setting of teacher-directed individual work. A typical example of this kind of setting at the preschool level would be the construction of a paper hatchet to commemorate Washington's birthday or the decoration of an egg to signify the approach of Easter. In this type of setting, the teacher generally controls the selection of materials to be used

60

(red and white construction paper), the selection and scheduling of activities (making a paper hatchet; "Anyone who isn't finished yet will have to put away their work until later, because we have to clean up now for snack"), and the selection and organization of procedures (cut, paste, color). The child is generally free to talk to, or ask the help of, other children around him, although the seating arrangement may have been originally planned by the teacher. This setting would be diagramed as follows:

SETTING: TEACHER-DIRECTED, INDIVIDUAL

Type of structure	Planning	Goal	Point on adaptation continuum
Selection and organization of objects	Conscious	Curriculum (learning to use various materials)	Near accommodation end
Selection and scheduling of activities	Conscious	Curriculum (reinforcing content taught)	Near accommodation end
Selection and organization of operations and procedures	Conscious	Curriculum-management (learning particular skills; doing what is manageable)	Near accommodation end
Selection of people with whom child interacts	Unconscious		Between midpoint and assimilation end

The educational consequence of this combination of structures would probably be that the inner-city child experiences failure and learns that he is inadequate, because he is again being asked to accommodate to several aspects of the situation at once. To provide a setting in which learning is more apt to occur, modification is again required.

In this instance, one might change the selection of materials so that the child has a choice between making a hatchet of paper or clay or pieces of wood, or perhaps, painting a hatchet. This type of structure would then move to a point between the midpoint and the assimilation end of the adaptation continuum. The rest of the diagram would be the same, because the child's choice of material would determine the operation or procedure to be used, and he would still be accommodating to that aspect of the situation. The educational consequence of this change is that some reinforcement of content occurs and the child learns new skills in handling art materials.

An alternative modification would be to allow the child to select the activity. He might decide to make a hatchet or he might decide to make a car or, perhaps, a free form. The selection of an activity would then be unconscious and would move to a point near the assimilation end of the adaptation continuum. The educational consequence of this modification would be that the child learns particular skills in handling a particular material. In either of these modifications the probability of the child's feeling successful is greatly increased, since he no longer has to produce something approaching the teacher's model.

The point of this whole discussion is that the teacher can control the combination of structures in any given setting so that the child meets a situation in which he must accommodate to something, but in which he is not required to make more accommodations than he can successfully handle. The background and experience of the child determine whether a particular object or operation requires adaptations in the form of accommodation or assimilation. As materials and procedures become familiar to children, they can more readily adapt to them by means that approach assimilation.

The obvious objection to the kinds of modification in settings that have been suggested above is that there aren't enough teachers to supervise such a variety of activities or materials at any one time. This is true. And this is why a successful program for inner-city children requires a low ratio of children to adults. For example, in the modified story-reading setting, one adult to three children would be a reasonable ratio if children are to be allowed to hear a story they prefer and to have an opportunity to make comments or raise questions. In the modified free-play setting, one adult to four or five children would provide reasonable assurance that all children are getting some social contact with an adult or some direction in alternative handling of objects.

Our recommendation is, therefore, that an adequate preschool program should maintain an adult-child ratio of one to four. A simple ratio, however, is not enough. What would happen in most Headstart programs is that five adults would work with all twenty children. For the inner-city child, who has not had much opportunity for verbal or physical interaction with adults, having to learn to interact with five different adults at once is a frightening task. It is little wonder that the child becomes "nonverbal." Given the same set of circumstances, many middle-class children would display the same kind of behavior.

We strongly suggest that at the beginning of the preschool or kindergarten program each adult should be assigned to work with a particular group of four children, and that the settings should consist mainly of modified free play, with some modified teacher-directed individual work. After several weeks for adjustment, the schedule should be modified so that any given group of four children would spend part of the day with another teacher. In this manner, the children would gradually learn to interact with all the adults. After the children have established a relationship with at least three of the adults in the classroom, modified group settings should be introduced and grouping of children can become more flexible.

ACHIEVING CONTENT GOALS

The modified settings that have been described above focus on particular "content" goals for the preschool and kindergarten child. These goals include the following:

1. Language development
   a. Learning to name new objects and new procedures
   b. Learning to talk to adults
   c. Learning to listen to others
   d. Learning to imitate more complex oral language
2. Manipulative skills
   a. Learning new ways of handling objects
   b. Learning new ways of combining objects to form new objects
3. Attitudes
   a. Learning to be successful in a school setting

The kinds of equipment that are selected and the ways in which this equipment is organized also contribute greatly to the content that is learned in a preschool or kindergarten program. Materials that develop hand-eye coordination or that lend themselves to various types of physical manipulations and arrangements are available and would be valuable. Hand puppets or family figures encourage many shy children to talk without feeling personal pressure. Full-length mirrors provide an opportunity for children to see themselves performing various activities, to become aware of their bodily movements, and to admire themselves. All of these responses are beneficial.

Equipment might well be reorganized periodically so that children become more aware of the various physical attributes that objects have. For example, construction paper that has been organized according to size might be reorganized according to color. Large blocks might be separated from small blocks, or hard (wooden) blocks might be separated from soft (foam) blocks. In this way, children can learn to accept various bases for organizing the objects in their environment.

In terms of the specific activities in which preschool and kindergarten children might engage, we should like to make a few suggestions. These are mainly activities that would be introduced in settings of teacher-directed group work or teacher-directed individual work; however, the materials should subsequently be made available to children who wish to continue the activity (or their own version of the activity) in the free-play setting.

LANGUAGE AND READING READINESS

The first activities we shall discuss relate to both language development and readiness for reading. One of the typical readiness experiences provided in kindergarten is to have children interpret pictures, telling a story about one picture or a series of sequential pictures. Sometimes they are asked to put a series of pictures in the appropriate sequence. For children who are unaccustomed to books, such pictures tend to represent static pieces of reality, it indeed they are seen as representing reality at all. Two sequential pictures are not seen as being related in time. The concept of such relationships between static representations is one that must be developed.

The inner-city child's world is one of action. Life is a series of moving images, and the major form of pictorial representation that he encounters at home is the television set, which also presents a moving image. The child must be helped to make the transition from moving images, where the transformations from one state to the next are visible, to static images, where the transformations must be imagined. Only then will pictures in books have real meaning for him.

To accomplish this, we suggest that a series of super-8 mm silent films be utilized. These can be produced by the local school to depict events that children would see in the area, such as a group of children playing a game of stick-ball, a fire truck rushing to a fire, or some adults having an argument. Each film would be about four minutes in length (one cartridge of film on a standard super-8 mm camera), and these films could be cartridged for use in Technicolor cartridge projectors, which are simple enough for children to operate themselves. A series of slides or still photographs would also be taken to correspond with each "story" on film. The equipment needed to produce these materials is not expensive, and no special skill is needed to operate the modern camera or to edit short films of this type.

Once produced, the films would be used in teacher-directed group settings to have children tell stories about what they see. After a film had been viewed and discussed two or three times, the slides or still photographs could be introduced and children would be asked to tell the story from these pictures. Finally, the still pictures could be "mixed up," and children could be asked to reconstruct the appropriate sequence. If still photographs are used, they can eventually be put on a series of charts to illustrate the children's story and to form a "Big Book."

Through this kind of activity, children can learn new words or phrases to use in talking about familiar events, they can learn the relationship between the static images in books and the moving images in the real world, and they can learn to be aware of sequences in time.

To give children more opportunity to talk about things and to learn new words, we suggest frequent trips. At least once a week preschool and kindergarten children should leave the school room and venture out into the world. These trips need not be elaborate, lengthy affairs, and they need *not* be all content oriented (such as visiting the fire house to learn about community helpers or visiting the zoo to learn about kinds of animals). A walk around the block to look for houses with black doors or windows with red curtains can be a learning experience in that it teaches children to observe details. A window-shopping tour of two or three stores provides topics for conversation and opportunity to learn new words. Watching a street-repair crew at work and, perhaps, talking to some of the men is also a valuable experience.

On trips of this nature, the whole class should not go to the same place at once. If five groups of children go to five different places or look for five different things on a walk around the block, then they have some "news" to tell each other when they get back to the classroom. On trips of this nature, Polaroid snapshots of things that are seen provide a reminder for children and stimulate later discussion.

Another important activity for language development and reading readiness is reading aloud to children. We suggested earlier that children should be allowed to choose the books they wish to hear. One way of handling this is to provide several books as possible choices. Children could then group themselves according to which book they wanted to hear, and several groups could be listening to different stories in different parts of the room. Stories should be repeated frequently. Indeed, a new book might well be reread for four or five consecutive days. It is only as a story becomes familiar to children that they can begin to inquire about it and play with it.

As a story becomes familiar, children should be encouraged to repeat sections of it (words or phrases or sentences) with the teacher as she reads it. In this way, new patterns of speaking become familiar to them. They should also be encouraged to raise questions about the story and to suggest alternative events; e.g., "What would happen to the egg if Horton-the-Elephant got off of Mayzie-the-Lazy-Bird's nest and went to play with his friends?" "What if Goldilocks came back to the three Bears' house some other time?" This kind of manipulation of a familiar story gives children a feeling that they can control the environment to some extent. A search for alternative endings helps to develop the attitude that reality can be changed, that they need not simply accept what is given; and this is an important attitude for inner-city children to have.

In addition, children will be learning to interact with the writer of a story. They will learn that what is written down in a book need not simply be accepted. The reader can think about what is said and can even disagree with it. Thus, at an early age, children are learning to become active readers rather than passive acceptors of the authority of the printed word.

MATHEMATICAL READINESS

The preschool and kindergarten program can also provide valuable experiences for developing mathematical readiness. The typical program already gives children experiences in counting that are related to daily activities, such as counting the number of children at a table and getting that many scissors or straws, etc. We suggest extending this type of activity to include measurements of various sorts.

Counting activities should include experience with various arrangements of objects. For example, if four children are seated at a table, they can be presented with four apples in a bowl. When children and apples have been counted, the teacher can ask whether each child will have an apple. Answers can be tested by distributing the apples. Next, the four apples can be placed in a row on the table, counted again, and the children asked whether there are more children or more apples. Again, their answers can be checked by distributing the apples. Various arrangements of the apples can be tried, using this pattern. An apple then can be added or taken away, the apples and children counted, and the children's ideas about equality tested again.

This procedure can be used with other kinds of materials, such as five paper bunnies and five paper carrots. In this case, each child can manipulate his own sets of objects, arranging them in space, counting them, matching them, and rearranging them and beginning again. Through experiences such as these, children begin to be aware that a group of four things can look bigger or smaller as they are arranged differently in space. They learn that counting and matching are ways of measuring numbers of objects. And they learn that adding or subtracting objects makes groups change in size or number.

Another activity that leads children to compare numbers is cardplaying. Preschool and kindergarten children can be provided with a "deck" of cards that has in it only aces, twos, and threes. Pairs of children can learn to play a simple matching game. Four cards are dealt to both players by A. A leads a card; B tries to beat it. If he can, he wins the two cards. If he can't, A wins the two cards. A and B both draw a new card. The winner leads the next card, and the game proceeds till all the cards are gone. When they first learn this game, the children will need to count the "spots" on the cards each time to see who has more spots. Gradually they will learn to recognize the number of spots immediately. As this happens, a new group of cards can be added to the deck—first fours, then fives, etc. Children's ability to recognize number groupings gradually increases in this way. Many children will learn to read number symbols through this simple activity. Even though the 2 printed on the card is never stressed, the child sees it in association with two spots and the spoken word "two."

Measurements of liquid and quantity can be encouraged through frequent cooking activities. Prepared foods make this a simple and relatively inexpensive procedure, and the product gives children nutritional value, as well as introducing them to new foods. Besides the traditional Jell-O or applesauce, children can use mixes to make instant puddings and cupcakes. They can be encouraged to experiment with the measurements. What happens to the Shake-a-Pudding if we use more water or less water than is called for by the recipe? In this way, the importance or value of measuring instruments can be impressed upon children.

A waterproof corner for experimentation in liquid measurement should be provided. Children should be encouraged to find out how many glasses of water must be used to fill a bowl up to the top. They can compare this with the number of pint milk cartons required to fill the same bowl. Other containers can be found in the room or brought from home to continue this type of testing. Charts or records can be kept by the children to indicate their findings, and experiments can be replicated by other children in the class.

Measurements of height might be based upon the young child's tendency to use himself as a measuring stick. Each child can be given a stick or length of heavy cardboard that matches his own height. He can then use this to measure the height of other objects in the room, including other people. Measurements can begin in a rough fashion, with things being labeled as *taller than, shorter than,* or *the same as.* Each child can keep his own list of items he has measured. These can be recorded with pictures or words or both, with the help of the teacher.

Gradually, the children can be introduced to a standard unit of measure and can learn how to compare heights to one unit or two units or three units of their standard. Their measurement of objects can be extended to length, using the same standard of measure. They can learn to test their measurements against those of other children in the class. Essentially, what they are learning is a new way of observing reality and of checking their observations against those of other people.

Another aspect of mathematical readiness that can be dealt with in the preschool and kindergarten program is the awareness of geometric forms. Young children differentiate between open and closed shapes fairly readily but may have difficulty in distinguishing one closed shape from another. Concrete models of the idealized geometric forms, such as the square, the triangle, the circle, the cube, the cone, and the sphere, should be available in the classroom. These can be compared to each other and to the objects in the classroom. Which objects resemble geometric combinations of shapes? Again, this type of activity encourages careful observation and gives children new categories with which to interpret reality and new words with which to talk about reality.

These are examples of some of the kinds of activities that can be provided for preschool and kindergarten children in an inner-city school. The emphasis is on giving them an opportunity to control some aspect of each activity, to have them learn through experimentation and through observations of concrete objects. In this way, they are learning to succeed in school at the same time that they are learning various student roles and various subject-matter content. This is a crucial aspect of a program for inner-city children.

THE KINDERGARTEN AND PRESCHOOL SCHEDULE

In this chapter we have not differentiated between the preschool program and the kindergarten program. We recommend that they should be organized in similar fashion. The major difference would be that children in the kindergarten would receive a half hour of perception training each day in a teacher-directed group-work setting. Otherwise, kindergarten would be a continuation of the preschool, building upon and extending the manipulative, language, and social skills already developed.

We recommend that the preschool and kindergarten classes run from 8 A.M. to 1 P.M., with a morning snack and a lunch period included. Each teacher or paraprofessional would work with only one class, with the exception of four paraprofessionals, trained in the perception program, who would spend a half hour with each of four kindergarten classes. During the afternoons, the preschool and kindergarten teachers can prepare materials, make home visits, work with paraprofessionals, and participate in the uncommon learning centers.

A sample schedule for a preschool class might be as follows:

8:00 A.M.	Free play and snack
	Children come in any time during the first hour and are permitted to eat their snack at any time during the hour. Teachers follow the modified free-play setting as outlined earlier.
9:00 A.M.	Teacher-directed group work
	This may be reading a story, for example.
9:30 A.M.	Gym or outdoor play
	An opportunity for active play. On occasion this may involve group games.
10:00 A.M.	Teacher-directed individual work
	This may be cooking or some other measuring activity. As children complete work it will dissolve gradually into . . . .
About 10:30 A.M.	Free play
	Children may continue some form of the previous activity or move to other activities of interest.
11:00 A.M.	Lunch
11:45 A.M.	Teacher-directed group work
	This might be a reading-readiness activity, such as viewing a film and discussing it.
12:15 or 12:30 P.M.	Teacher-directed individual work
	This could involve art work or construction work of some type. It could be related to the theme of the film that has been discussed.
1:00 P.M.	Home

The kindergarten classes would be scheduled along similar lines, except that the teacher-directed settings would be moved about to enable the paraprofessionals to work with all classes.

A preschool class should consist of about twenty children and five teachers. If a preschool program does not exist in a particular school, then the kindergarten class should operate under this ratio of twenty children and five teachers. If the kindergarten group has had prior experience in a preschool program, then a kindergarten class can probably operate effectively with twenty children and three teachers in addition to the paraprofessionals working in the perception program.

	8:00 to 9:00 A.M.	9:00 to 9:30	9:30 to 10:00	10:00 to 10:30	10:30 to 11:00	11:00 to 11:45	11:45 to 12:15 P.M.	12:15 to 1:00
Class A	Free play and snack	T-D Group work in perception	T-D Individual work	Free play	Gym or outdoor play	Lunch	T-D Group work	T-D Individual work
Class B	Free play and snack	T-D Individual work	T-D Group work in perception	Free play	Gym or outdoor play	Lunch	T-D Group work	T-D Individual work
Class C	Free play and snack	T-D Individual work	Free play	Gym or outdoor play	T-D Group work in perception	Lunch	T-D Group work	T-D Individual work
Class D	Free play and snack	T-D Group work	T-D Individual work	Gym or outdoor play	Free play	Lunch	T-D Group work in perception	T-D Individual work

At least two of the teachers in a preschool or kindergarten class should be regularly trained and certified professionals. The others may be paraprofessionals trained to work in the various kinds of preschool activities suggested earlier in this chapter. We strongly suggest that some of these paraprofessionals should be young men or boys in their late teens. Children at this age respond favorably to males, although in the early grades the school rarely allows them much contact with men. Given the family structure of the inner-city child and the lack of a father in many homes, it would seem important to provide young children with masculine contacts in school.

SUMMARY

To summarize briefly, the preschool and kindergarten program aims at helping children to learn to play various student roles, to learn particular kinds of content, and to develop certain positive attitudes toward themselves and toward school. The program is adapted to the particular needs of the inner-city child by modifying certain aspects of the traditional preschool settings so that the child maintains some decision-making power at the same time that he is being asked to adapt to new procedures or materials. This modification of settings, in turn, requires some modification in the adult-child ratio and in grouping practices.

As a whole, the preschool and kindergarten program is designed to provide a foundation for the curriculum that the child will meet in the first and second grade.

SIX: FORMING BASIC MATHEMATICAL CONCEPTS

To teach mathematics effectively to young children (ages 5, 6, and 7), several propositions must be kept in mind. First, it must be remembered that the young child learns through constantly interacting with the environment. He may memorize that five plus five equals ten and if asked, "What is five plus five?" he may well tell you "Ten"; but it would be a mistake to conclude that he knows what "five" means or what "plus" means or what "equals" or "ten" means. As far as the child knows, it is all gibberish. What number concepts the child learns must be learned through examining concrete materials. What concepts of addition, subtraction, multiplication, or division he develops must be learned through manipulative action. In short, elements to be learned must be concretely represented, and operations to be learned must be acted out physically.

The child does have, however, some abilities that enable him to function with these concrete materials and in so doing to learn mathematics. One, he has learned to physically grasp and manipulate objects. Two, he has learned to connect language to physical events and actions. Three, he has learned to communicate using language. Four, he can listen. Five, he can observe. Six, he is in the process of developing the ability to classify through grouping objects together according to some attribute that they all have in common. Seven, he is developing the ability to order objects according to size or some other aspect in which the objects differ. In short, he is beginning to see relations, such as A is larger than B, X is the father of Y. Eight, the child is beginning to put things into one-to-one correspondence. He may, for example, match one knife and one fork to each plate at the table. Nine, the child assumes or has learned that there is some stability in the world. If you say your name is Mary, he doesn't assume that your name will change in the next ten minutes. If ☼ is called "apple" now, it won't be called "house" later. If it is, the child says there is an error someplace.

Given, then, that the child has certain logical and physical abilities that enable him to begin to classify and order concrete reality in particular ways, certain linguistic abilities that enable him to talk about what he does and sees, and the ability to observe and listen to others as they classify, order, and talk about the concrete reality with which they are dealing, and given, further, that the child learns through these activities, the role of those who would teach the child is to set up experiences involving the child with concrete realities that have in them the concepts one wishes to teach. If at first reading this all seems complicated to the uninitiated, it should be kept in mind that learning is a complicated process. It is not so complicated, however, that one cannot set up experiences for children from which they can learn what is intended. It is the children who have to do the hard work of learning. Though, in truth, they invariably view real learning as a game.

SAMPLE LESSONS IN MATHEMATICAL CONCEPTS

In an effort to make matters more clear, let us describe a lesson that any reasonably mature person can try out with a 5- or 6-year-old, a lesson that leads to the learning of mathematics and that helps to develop the logical abilities of children.

Sit at a table with the child and the following materials: five pennies, five quarters, five matchsticks. Proceed as follows: Set the quarters and the matchsticks aside. Uncover one penny from under your left hand and tell the child, "Here is one penny." Uncover two pennies from under your right hand and say, "Here are two pennies." Pointing to each pile in turn, say, "Here is one penny; here are two pennies." Cover them up. Lift the left hand and ask, "How many?" If the response is correct, lift the right hand and ask, "How many are here?" If the response is incorrect, say, "No," and take one penny and place it toward the center of the table. Place two pennies approximately 8 inches to the right of the single penny. Place a quarter 8 inches below the single penny and two quarters 8 inches below the two pennies. Place a single matchstick 8 inches below the two quarters. Point to the matchstick and say, "Here is one matchstick. Here is one quarter." Pointing to the lone penny, ask, "How many pennies are here?" You will probably get "One" for an answer, as the answer was given correctly earlier. Then pointing, observe, "Here are two matchsticks. Here are two quarters." Pointing to the two pennies, ask, "How many pennies are here?" The child will now probably give the correct response. Should he be unable to do so, get three spoons, three knives, three plates, three needles and set them up with the pennies, quarters, and matchsticks in the same arrangement. As you point to the objects, say, "Here is one knife. Here are two knives. Here is one fork. Here are two forks. Here is one needle. Here are two needles. Here is one plate. Here are two plates. Here is one matchstick." Pointing to the two matchsticks, ask, "How many matchsticks are here?" If answered correctly, point to the two quarters and ask, "How many quarters are here?" If the child answers, "Two," point to the single quarter, the single penny, and the pair of pennies, each time asking the appropriate question.

Clear the table and, with your hands under the table, place two pennies under the left hand and one under the right. Lift the left hand and ask, "How many are here?" Get the child's response. If correct, lift the right hand and repeat the question. Once the child demonstrates that he can identify correctly the number of pennies no matter where they are placed, put two pennies under the right hand and three under the left hand. Say, "How many are under this hand?" as you lift your right hand. If the response is correct, lift the left hand and tell the child, "There are three pennies here." Ask him to say, "Three." After the child repeats "Three," cover and uncover the three pennies and ask him, "How many?"

See if he can take three forks out of the drawer. See if he can take two matchsticks and three quarters from the objects on the table. Put two quarters under one hand and three under the other and ask the question, "How many?" of each group.

Put one quarter under one hand and two under the other. If the child correctly identifies the number under each hand as the coins are uncovered, push the one quarter over next to the two quarters, cover them, and ask if he knows how many quarters are under the hand. After he responds, uncover the coins and ask if he is correct. If the child is being highly successful, stay very briefly with the quarters, and then move to the matchsticks. If the child is not having a great deal of success, switch the game as follows. Give the child three quarters or three pennies. Tell him he is the teacher. He is to put one, two, or three pennies under his hand and is then to lift his hand and ask you, "How many are there?" You will play the student and give an answer. He may or may not tell you if you are right, but he must tell you if you are wrong.

The benefits of playing this game, which we shall call for the purposes of identification the "You're-the-Teacher" game, are several. Learning is largely a business of the learner settling an issue of doubt. Human beings, by nature, like to resolve doubt—to come to a feeling of certainty. In order to reach certainty, the individual must find some answer that he feels removes the doubt in such a way that he now sees it "like it is." The child with whom you have been working and who is failing rather consistently to give correct answers undoubtedly has learned some things. He has learned that there is a problem that has to do with relating certain language (one, two, three) to the pennies you uncover each time. Further, each time there is a difference in what is uncovered. Undoubtedly, the child has some hypothesis about what words go with what combinations, but unfortunately, you are setting up the order of events. In short, you are controlling the situation. By playing the You're-the-Teacher game, you shift the control to the child. The basic problem or doubt that faces the child, plus the way you have structured the game, plus the hypothesis he wishes to test give all the direction that is needed to the child. Furthermore, if he hasn't been doing too well up to this point, by placing him in the role of teacher, you have greatly reduced his chances of failing. He can now ask questions, which is a legitimate function of the role he is playing— the teacher—and not be held responsible for the answers, as they are your responsibility.

In playing the game, many children will first test you by giving you problems to which they already know the answer. In this way they can see if you are going to give them correct answers or if you are going to try and be tricky. Give them the correct answers. After they feel confident that you are giving them correct answers (you have just answered the same question correctly six times), they will begin trying to remove their doubts by hypothesis testing. Some will be more systematic than others, but all will test hypotheses. They may have a hypothesis that the correct response to OOO is "Two," so they will test it by giving you the problem. When you say "Three," they will offer you OO, to which you respond "Two." At this point they may give you OO again. They will then offer you OOO until such time as they are confident that they have solved the problem. At this point you may test them by offering some wrong responses.

It may also be at this point that children will switch to quarters or matchsticks or a combination of these. This is good. They may even add a fourth penny and a fifth penny. All this indicates that they have resolved the original problem that faced them and feel confident enough to move on to another problem. Significantly, they also feel that they have a method for resolving the problem. Play the game for as long as they will. In the process, they may discover that O plus OO is another way of saying OOO.

In the event that the child doesn't get to "One plus two equals three," or in the event that he moves to correctly naming groups of one, two, three, four, and five without the game, proceed as follows. Say to the child, "Here is one penny in front of my left hand, and here are two in front of my right hand. I'm going to push the two pennies in front of my right hand over next to the penny in front of my left hand. Now how many pennies are in front of my left hand?" When the child responds, "Three," say, "Yes, one plus two equals three."

Next, place two pennies in front of your left hand and two pennies in front of your right hand. Pointing to those in front of your left hand, ask, "How many are here?" Then, pointing to those in front of the right hand, "How many are here?" Next, push the two pennies in front of the right hand over with those in front of the left hand. Ask, "How many do we now have?" When you get a response of "Four," say, "Yes, two plus two equals four." Follow the same procedure with one and three, three and one, one and two, etc.

Several things should be kept in mind while doing these exercises. First, it is important that there be no confusion in the child's mind about how many pennies are four pennies. If you have doubt as to how sure the child is, put nine or ten pennies in a group on the table and ask the child to place four pennies in his hand or to give you four pennies—or three pennies or two or whatever concept you wish to test. It is important that the child know these concepts of number if you are to reduce confusion in your addition lesson. It is the certainty of knowing that OOOO is "four" and OOO is "three" that enables the child to move to the uncertainty of what "plus" and "equals" means.

Second, keep in mind that "equals" is the proper mathematical term. "One and three are four" is nonsense. One and three are one and three, and four is four, not one and three. Not to recognize this is to confuse further what is already an uncertain situation.

Third, remember to use the term "plus," as later you will use the plus sign (+) in writing, not an "added to" sign or an "and" sign. If the child views + as "and," well and good. Operationally he will see + as the act of combining or adding to, but it should also be noted that mathematics is a precise language and the precise term is "plus." From the beginning, the child will do well to be exposed to precise language.

Once a child has the concepts of "one," "two," "three," and "four" and he is able to state such number facts as $1 + 3 = 4$, $3 + 1 = 4$, and $2 + 2 = 4$, the person doing the teaching needs to move to extend these concepts and facts. The concept of "zero" and the facts $0 + 0 = 0$, $0 + 1 = 1$, $1 + 0 = 1$, $0 + 2 = 2$, $2 + 0 = 2$, $0 + 3 = 3$, $3 + 0 = 3$, $0 + 4 = 4$, and $4 + 0 = 4$ can be taught quickly by showing a child an empty hand and asking, "How many pennies do I have in my hand?" The child will say, "None," or, "Silly, you don't have no pennies," or something of this nature. Your response is to say, "Yes, I have zero pennies. How many dogs are sitting on the table?"

CHILD: None.
TEACHER: Yes, zero dogs. How many matchsticks do I have in this hand?
CHILD: None.
TEACHER: Yes, zero. Can you say zero?
CHILD: Zero.
TEACHER: What does zero mean?
CHILD: None.
TEACHER: Yes, mathematicians use the term or word "zero" to mean none.

74

That the child is not clear as to what "mathematicians" means shouldn't worry us. It is, after all, what we are teaching him.

Once the child can handle $0 + 1 = 1$, $2 + 0 = 2$, $3 + 0 = 3$, etc., he may well verbalize the proposition that zero plus any other number is equal to that number (the identity property). It is well to note, however, that children will often learn this proposition operationally before they can verbalize it. For example, a teacher asks a child the following problem: "Suppose there was a number called *glump* and you had the problem, 'Zero plus glump equals _____.' What would the answer be?" The child might well respond correctly with the answer, "Glump."

Everyone would probably infer from this that the child understands what the result is when you add zero to any number. This doesn't mean, however, that the child can construct and verbally present the proposition or statement that "Zero plus any number equals that number." Nor will asking the child why the answer is "glump" help a great deal, as the child who has yet to form the proposition verbally will, at best, say, "Because you added zero to it." If you say, "But why should that make any difference?" he is likely to say, "Because." Children eventually will get around to verbalizing these statements. If the teacher is patient and keeps offering problems that illustrate the principle, he will be doing about all he can do.

For the teacher to verbalize the proposition will only waste time, unless he is teaching a parrot. Children will parrot also. Perhaps the chief failure of the schools has been that they have produced a nation of parrots who speak words but don't see any connection between the words and the reality in which they live. Let the child first understand concrete reality. Let him manipulate it. As he manipulates it, you can judge if he understands it. Then, and only then, let him talk about that reality and the process of manipulating it. You won't be fooled if you follow this rule. If, on the other hand, you have a lot of propositions memorized by children, you will be hard put to know if they really know anything about the reality you are talking about or if they can manipulate it meaningfully.

Besides developing the concept "zero," you will need to develop the concepts "five," six," "seven," "eight," "nine," and "ten." The related addition facts also need to be developed. If the child learns in the morning that OOOOO is "five," then in the afternoon he can be taught $0 + 5$, $5 + 0$, $1 + 4$, $4 + 1$, $3 + 2$, and $2 + 3$ by the method suggested above. Some of the children who are getting the game quickly may be able to figure these matters out for themselves, and they may well begin to ask, "How much is five plus one or five plus two." This reveals a great deal of insight on the part of the child into the nature of the number system.

In order to foster the insight that one more can always be added, it is a good idea to introduce a number by putting before the child the largest group he has learned to date. A sample lesson with a student named Ed might proceed as follows:

1. TEACHER: How many pennies are here?
2. If five, child will say, "Five."

The teacher is making sure the child knows "five." One can also check this out by placing the various groups of objects before the child and asking about them.

3. TEACHER: Yes. Now I want you to add one penny to the group so that we will have six pennies in the group.
4. TEACHER: Okay. How many pennies are in the group?

The teacher is showing what "six" would look like.

5. ED: Six.

The teacher gives the child experience saying "six."

6. TEACHER: Take one away. How many are in the group now?
7. ED: Five.

The teacher is introducing notion of subtraction, which is the physical removal of the penny. The teacher is also moving the child back to the known.

8. TEACHER: Okay, put back the penny you took away. Now how many are there?
9. ED: Six.

The teacher wants to get the child back to the notion of "six" while it is fresh in the child's mind. He also introduces the idea that $5 + 1 = 6$. Note: If the child has trouble here, steps 4 through 9 can be repeated.

10. TEACHER: Here, add this penny to the group. How many are there now? Don't know? Okay, there are seven. How many?
11. ED: Seven.
12. TEACHER: Yes. How many?
13. ED: Seven.

Concept of "seven" is introduced, and $6 + 1 = 7$ is introduced. Practice in using the term "seven" is required.

14. TEACHER: Take one away. How many now?
15. ED: Six.
16. TEACHER: Put one back. How many now?
17. ED: Seven.
18. TEACHER: Take one away.
19. ED: Six.
20. TEACHER: Put one back.
21. ED: Seven.
22. TEAGHER: Take one away.
23. ED: Six.

The teacher is giving the child opportunities to learn something of the concepts "six" and "seven." The child also is getting an opportunity to learn or discover that $6 + 1 = 7$ and $7 - 1 = 6$.

24. TEACHER: Take one away and how many are there?
25. ED: Five.
26. TEACHER: Add one.

27. ED: Six.
28. TEACHER: Add one.
29. ED: Seven.
30. TEACHER: Subtract one.
31. ED: Six.
32. TEACHER: Add one.
33. ED: Seven.

The teacher is giving Ed opportunities to see that five holds the same relation to six as six does to seven. In dialogue 30, the teacher is introducing the term "subtract." In this sequence, the teacher is also beginning to work on the notion that subtraction undoes addition.

34. TEACHER: Subtract one.
35. ED: Six.
36. TEACHER: Subtract one.
37. ED: Five.
38. TEACHER: Subtract one.
39. ED: Four.
40. TEACHER: Subtract one.
41. ED: Three.
42. TEACHER: Subtract one.
43. ED: Two.
44. TEACHER: Subtract one.
45. ED: One.
46. TEACHER: Subtract one.
47. ED: None.
48. TEACHER: No.
49. ED: Zero.
50. TEACHER: Add one.
51. ED: One.
52. TEACHER: Add one.
53. ED: Two.
54. TEACHER: Add one.
55. ED: Three.
56. TEACHER: Add one.
57. ED: Four.
58. TEACHER: Add one.
59. ED: Five.
60. TEACHER: Add one.
61. ED: Six.
62. TEACHER: Add one.
63. ED: Seven.

The teacher is working on the notion of counting and order, as well as laying the groundwork for concept of infinity. Neither of these notions will be fully appreciated in this lesson. The child is also getting opportunities to see the consequences of adding or subtracting one.

64. TEACHER: Subtract two.
65. ED: Five.

77

66. TEACHER: Subtract two.
67. ED: Three.
68. TEACHER: Subtract two.
69. ED: One.
70. TEACHER: Add one.
71. ED: Two.
72. TEACHER: Add one.
73. ED: Three.
74. TEACHER: Add two.
75. ED: Five.
76. TEACHER: Add two.
77. ED: Seven.
78. TEACHER: Subtract one.
79. ED: Six.
80. TEACHER: Subtract two.
81. ED: Four.
82. TEACHER: Subtract two.
83. ED: Two.
84. TEACHER: Subtract two.
85. ED: Zero.
86. TEACHER: Add two.
87. ED: Two.
88. TEACHER: Subtract two.
89. ED: Zero.

Ed is getting opportunity to extend knowledge of two and see the relative power of one to two while getting additional practice on number facts.

90. TEACHER: Add three.
91. ED: Three.
92. TEACHER: Subtract two.
93. ED: One.
94. TEACHER: Add three.
95. ED: Four.
96. TEACHER: Add two.
97. ED: Six.
98. TEACHER: Add one.
99. ED: Seven.
100. TEACHER: Subtract two.
101. ED: Five.
102. TEACHER: Add one.
103. ED: Six.

The teacher is offering a variety of problems that primarily give practice on some of the facts and that break what was getting to be too stylized and routinized—in short, changing the pace.

104. TEACHER: Subtract three.
105. ED: Three.
106. TEACHER: Subtract three.
107. ED: Zero.
108. TEACHER: Add three.

109. ED: Three.
110. TEACHER: Add three.
111. ED: Six.
112. TEACHER: Subtract three.
113. ED: Three.
114. TEACHER: Subtract three.
115. ED: Zero.
116. TEACHER: Add three.
117. ED: Three.
118. TEACHER: Add three.
119. ED: Six.
120. TEACHER: Subtract one.

Dialogue 120 is a transition to the following:

121. ED: Five
122. TEACHER: Subtract three.
123. ED: Two.
124. TEACHER: Add three.
125. ED: Five.
126. TEACHER: Subtract three.
127. ED: Two.
128. TEACHER: Add three.
129. ED: Five.
130. TEACHER: Subtract two.
131. ED: Three.
132. TEACHER: Add two.
133. ED: Five.
134. TEACHER: Subtract two.
135. ED: Three.
136. TEACHER: Add two.
137. ED: Five.
138. TEACHER: Subtract three.
139. ED: Two.

Instance of relationship of addition to subtraction is shown again with numbers five, three, and two. Experiences are given with number facts $2 + 3$, $3 + 2$, $5 - 2$, and $5 - 3$.

140. TEACHER: Add five.
141. ED: Seven.
142. TEACHER: Subtract five.
143. ED: Two.
144. TEACHER: Add five.
145. ED: Seven.
146. TEACHER: Subtract five.
147. ED: Two.
148. TEACHER: Add five.
149. ED: Seven.
150. TEACHER: Subtract two
151. ED: Five.

152. TEACHER: Add two.
153. ED: Seven.
154. TEACHER: Subtract two.
155. ED: Five.
156. TEACHER: Add two.
157. ED: Seven.

Experiences of the same kind are given for two, five, and seven.

158. TEACHER: Subtract six.
159. ED: One.
160. TEACHER: Add six.
161. ED: Seven.
162. TEACHER: Subtract six.
163. ED: One.
164. TEACHER: Add six.
165. ED: Seven.
166. TEACHER: Subtract six.
167. ED: One.
168. TEACHER: Add six.
169. ED: Seven.
170. TEACHER: Subtract six.
171. ED: One.

Similar experiences given for one, six, and seven.

172. TEACHER: Add five.
173. ED: Six.
174. TEACHER: Subtract four.
175. ED: Two.
176. TEACHER: Add four.
177. ED: Six.
178. TEACHER: Subtract four.
179. ED: Two.
180. TEACHER: Add four.
181. ED: Five.
182. TEACHER: Here are two other pennies. Add three to them.
183. ED: Five.
184. TEACHER: What happened?
185. ED: I made a mistake. The answer to the other problem is six.

Experiences are given with two, four, and six.

186. TEACHER: Okay. Clear the table and put two pennies out front. Add two.
187. ED: Four.
188. TEACHER: Add three.
189. ED: Seven.
190. TEACHER: Add one. That makes eight.
191. TEACHER: Subtract one.
192. ED: Seven.
193. TEACHER: Add one.
194. ED: Eight.
195. TEACHER: Subtract two.

80

196. ED: Six.
197. TEACHER: Add two.
198. ED: Eight.
199. TEACHER: Subtract one.
200. ED: Seven.
201. TEACHER: Add one.
202. ED: Eight.
203. TEACHER: Subtract two.
204. ED: Six.
205. TEACHER: Add two.
206. ED: Eight.
207. TEACHER: Subtract three.
208. ED: Five.
209. TEACHER: Add three.
210. ED: Eight.
211. TEACHER: Subtract three.
212. ED: Five.
213. TEACHER: Subtract one.
214. ED: Four.
215. TEACHER: Add four.
216. ED: Eight.
217. TEACHER: Subtract four.
218. ED: Four.
219. TEACHER: Add four.
220. ED: Eight.
221. TEACHER: Subtract five.
222. ED: Three.
223. TEACHER: Add five.
224. ED: Eight.
225. TEACHER: Subtract six.
226. ED: Two.
227. TEACHER: Add six.
228. ED: Eight.
229. TEACHER: Subtract seven.
230. ED: One.
231. TEACHER: Add seven.
232. ED: Eight.
233. TEACHER: Subtract eight.
234. ED: Zero.
235. TEACHER: Add eight.
236. ED: Eight.

Experiences are given that help Ed to make sure of his number facts and that will reveal the relationships between one, two, three, four, five, six, seven, and eight. At Dialogue 189, a task is given that introduces the new number "eight." This should be done with a minimum of fuss. The child probably doesn't know the answer. The teacher should simply supply the answer and assume the child will know how to handle the new number from his previous learnings of how he handled "five," "six," and "seven" as they were introduced. This assumption is much more flattering to children than a lot of verbal praise. Too much verbal praise over each new learning leads children to the belief that down deep teachers think they are basically stupid. The child, on the other hand, feels that if he has demonstrated that he could handle seven previous numbers that the teacher ought to believe in him enough to know that he can handle the eighth. Furthermore, children come to believe that good teachers introduce concepts they feel their students can handle.

237. TEACHER: Okay. Any comments or questions on what we have done?
238. ED: . . . .

Dialogue 238 may be a smile or a long discourse. Keep comments at a minimum if a long discourse is given. Ask questions and be supportive. Keep in mind what you want to accomplish with this child and respond accordingly.

The dialogues above are in the teacher's mind at the start of the lesson in a loose kind of order. The teacher has certain sequences in mind, and he has in mind an order for the sequences. How often he uses a sequence or the actual order in which the sequences are used is a function of how the child is responding. How sure are the answers, how quick are they coming, what asides are being made, what errors are being made? The game is to adjust the sequences and their order to the particular child.

In our dialogue we have included only one error on the part of the child. How a teacher handles an error is of some importance. The teacher will, for the most part, recognize immediately that an error has been made. The child may not recognize it at all. The teacher's job is not so much to tell the child he has made an error as to set up a situation in which the *child* recognizes that one has been made and corrects it. In the instance above in Dialogues 179 through 186, the teacher has simply had the child set up the problem $2 + 3$ next to the problem $2 + 4$ on which the error was made. The child sees that he is asserting that $2 + 4 = 5$ and $2 + 3 = 5$. Most children will quickly see that this cannot be the case and will check their work for the error. If the error is not seen, the teacher can capitalize on the experiences the child has had with the relationship of addition to subtraction. The teacher could say: "Put six pennies on the table. Subtract four. What is the answer?" The child will say, "Two." He is now faced with asserting that $2 + 4 = 5$, $2 + 3 = 5$, and $6 - 4 = 2$. The first two suggest that something is wrong. The third example suggests a solution.

It is important, both from the standpoint of the child's self-concept and from the standpoint of teaching children the intellectual rules of the game, that the child discover his errors and make or work out the solutions. The teacher's job is to manipulate the data so that a contradiction is seen. If the teacher is not the authority for truth in mathematics, we must be careful that he is not the authority for falsity. Truth and falsity rest with the data, the senses, and the rules of the game.

82

TIMING OF LESSONS

Let us pause here and make some observations on the above lesson or lessons. The notion of a lesson that is planned for twenty minutes or thirty minutes, in which a teacher sets out to develop a specific point or points, doesn't work too well. Our own view is to start a lesson and go. To guess how far one can go in twenty minutes or thirty minutes is foolish. The actual doing will give the answer. To predict a period of time for which a child will work and pay attention is also useless. We have seen 3-year-olds pay attention to lessons of the "how-many-pennies" type long enough to exhaust most adults. Our view is to teach the lesson. If it's not going well, stop. There's always later. Lessons can fail to succeed for lots of reasons, and it makes little sense to us to force them. Begging the children to go on because it is good for them or because it will make the teacher happy makes the least sense.

On the other hand, given the many reasons why a lesson may not go or succeed, it makes little sense to us to stop a lesson that is going well. If children are firing back correct answers, handling operations, asking questions, learning, filling the air with the excitement of the moment's challenge, then forget about naptime. It can wait. Our business as teachers is answers, operations, questions, learning, excitement — not milk or naps.

We once taught mathematics for a week to a first-grade class for a solid hour prior to milk time. The children did not want to stop. The school rule that said the children should have milk at ten o'clock stopped the lesson each day. The regular classroom teacher reported that some of the children were tired after our lesson and took naps during milk break. We asked how they performed after milk break. She reported, "The same as always." We suppose this proves that when a child is in a learning situation that is exciting, it takes a great deal of energy. Learning is work and it's exciting and it tires a fellow out. The children don't complain, and short naps put them back in business. Most children, however, are willing to take the excitement now and the nap a little later.

Another view of a lesson is that the lesson is mathematics. Cut the above lesson up into one, two, three, or more segments and it's pretty much the same lesson. Given a child and a teacher of unlimited energy, interest, and no outside interference, in one lesson all of mathematics could be taught. Mathematics is a total living thing, not a series of lessons. The concept of "lesson" is artificial and arbitrary. This may explain why many lessons are artificial and arbitrary.

In the lesson above, at one point the questions begin to go unsaid. This comes through a mutual, but unstated, agreement between teacher and student. This is done to speed the lesson on its way. Speed is important for two reasons, each having to do with maximizing learning. First, the closer in time you can place two events, the more likely the learner is to make a connection between the two events. Second, as a general rule, the more data with which one has to work, the more likely one is to arrive at sound conclusions. If

$7 - 2 = 5$ and $5 + 2 = 7$ are fifteen minutes apart in time, with sixty other events intervening, the child will be hard pressed to see that subtraction is the inverse of addition. If, however, they are close to each other in time, so that the one hits the mind before the other is gone, the chances of seeing the connection are greatly increased. Further — and this is our second point — if $7 - 2 = 5$ and $5 + 2 = 7$ is followed by $8 - 2 = 6$ and $6 + 2 = 8$ and $7 - 3 = 4$ and $4 + 3 = 7$ plus thirteen other like examples, all in a relatively short period of time, the large number of examples again increases the chance of the child seeing that subtraction undoes addition and vice versa.

Too often children are asked to generalize in data-poor situations. Teachers who have had fifty instances of some principle finally see the principle. They then see that one or two instances are enough to arrive logically at the principle. Logically, yes. Psychologically, no. If the principle could be seen by everyone with one, two, or three instances, why didn't the teacher see it with only two or three instances? Perhaps it is because it is only after we clearly see the principle that we clearly see the problem. The child doesn't know the problem is there. He becomes aware of it gradually. In the indeterminate learning situation it is not just the principle that we don't know, it is often the problem.

In connection with the above, there is another reason for including a great deal of data in each lesson. Underlying each number fact and each operation are powerful intellectual ideas. In the lesson above, the following notions lay buried: addition, subtraction, the relationship of addition to subtraction, commutativity, concept of number, counting, identity property, and the concept of infinity. Each of these notions will appear over and over again in lesson after lesson. Eventually, the child will see them if he is given enough data and if the data are organized in a way that will increase the chances of his seeing the ideas embedded in the data. We shall return to the question of order in a moment.

Before looking at order, let us observe that while we are moving the child along as rapidly as we can, the child is also in control of the rate with which we move. We cannot confront the child with too many data at one time or too many questions at one time or he will become overwhelmed. Therefore, the child can slow us down or speed us up by delaying the answer or by giving it to us quickly. The child also controls the pace by the speed with which he physically adds or subtracts the pennies.

Some children may move away from the physical moving of pennies into and out of the group and handle the problem intellectually. This is desirable but should not be commented upon by the teacher. If the teacher says, "Very good, you no longer need to physically move the pennies. You can do the problems in your head," the child may not go back to physically manipulating the coins when he gets stuck or is unsure of an answer. The reason for this is that he doesn't want to take a step backwards. In his comment, the teacher taught the child that mental manipulation is superior to physical manipulation which, of course, it isn't. The way that most effectively removes doubt from the child's mind is the best way. Of course, eventually the child will more and more work without the physical activity simply because it is quicker, and human beings in our culture like to do some things the quickest way in order to make time for other things. The point we wish to emphasize is that the child has learned the operation as a physical operation, and through the speed with which he works, he controls the speed with which we can move him along.

Further, we should emphasize that in learning the physical operation the child has been given a means of demonstrating his answers. He can show you that he had six, removed one, and now has five. His senses confirm what he is telling you. Answers arrived at through mental operations without appeal to the concrete reality of a situation must be defended with verbal logic. This, the child handles poorly, at best. Some skeptics feel that this is why teachers prefer mental operations with concrete reality absent. It leaves truth in the hands of the authoritarian teacher and not in the senses of the child. Truth is "Teacher says so," not "Look, I can show you. See for yourself." One learns blind faith with this kind of teaching and is trained for demagoguery.

When the child can control the pace and when he has a means of working out his answers that enables him to see the truth of what he is saying, his self-concept is enhanced. It is enhanced because he sees that he is solving problems, he sees he is learning. He knows he's not stupid. And success by students breeds more success.

MATHEMATICAL EXERCISES

Let us now extend our lesson. To date we have been working with addition and subtraction facts through eight. An exercise that is helpful at this point is the following. Construct a series of plain 12- by 18-inch sheets of paper that look as follows:

```
+        =
+        =
+        =
+        =
+        =
+        =
+        =
+        =
```

Using tokens, have the children construct all the statements that use two elements and that equal one, two, three, four, five, six, seven, and eight. They will physically construct each of these statements by placing the tokens in the proper places. The sheets would look like those below. The absence of any tokens in a position signifies zero.

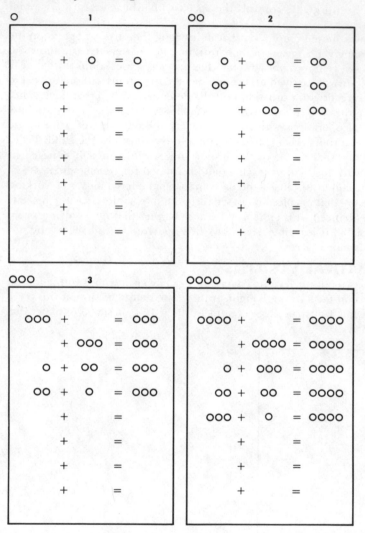

As the child completes each of these number families, he should be asked to read the results to an adult. The one for number three he would read as follows: "Three plus zero equals three; zero plus three equals three; one plus two equals three; two plus one equals three."

The instructions to the child are to find all of the combinations that add up to the number in question. He does this by placing the tokens to the left and to the right of the plus sign. This he should do readily, as it only requires an extension of his previous experience. No two facts or statements should be alike. The column after the equal sign will, of course, always have the same number of tokens in each statement.

OOOOO   5

OOOOO +		= OOOOO
	+ OOOOO	= OOOOO
O +	OOOO	= OOOOO
OO +	OOO	= OOOOO
OOO +	OO	= OOOOO
OOOO +	O	= OOOOO
+		=
+		=

OOOOOO   6

+ OOOOOO	=	OOO OOO
O + OOOOO	=	OOO OOO
OO + OOOO	=	OOO OOO
OOO + OOO	=	OOO OOO
OOOO + OO	=	OOO OOO
OOOOO + O	=	OOO OOO
OOO OOO +	=	OOO OOO
+	=	

OOOOOOO   7

OOO OOOO +	=	OOO OOOO
+ OOO OOOO	=	OOO OOOO
OOO OOO + O	=	OOO OOOO
O + OOO OOO	=	OOO OOOO
OO OOO + OO	=	OOO OOOO
OO + OO OOO	=	OOO OOOO
OOOO + OOO	=	OOO OOOO
OOO + OOOO	=	OOO OOOO

OOOOOOOO   8

OOO OOO + OO	=	OOOO OOOO
OOOO + OOOO	=	OOOO OOOO
OOOO OOOO +	=	OOOO OOOO
O + OOOO OOO	=	OOOO OOOO
OO + OOO OOO	=	OOOO OOOO
OOO + OOOOO	=	OOOO OOOO
OOOOO + OOO	=	OOOO OOOO
+ OOOO OOOO	=	OOOO OOOO
OOO OOOO + O	=	OOOO OOOO

Some children will discover, after doing the first four or five, that they can predict how many statements will be needed to complete the next one and that there is in fact an arithmetic progression.

87

Observant teachers can also note if the children are becoming more logical or if they are working rather randomly. If one looks at the above exercise for the number six, he sees that the child has systematically increased the left side by one each time and reduced the right side by one. This is a good sign. The teacher may also see the recognition on the part of a child of some mathematical property. In the exercise for the number seven, for example, we see that the child has discovered the property of commutativity. She has combined the notion of order and the property of commutativity by starting with $7 + 0$ and commuting to get $0 + 7$. She then subtracts one from the left and adds it to the right to get $6 + 1$. She commutes to get $1 + 6$. She subtracts one again from the right and adds one to the left to get $5 + 2$. Again she commutes to get $2 + 5$. She then moves to $4 + 3$ and $3 + 4$ by the same strategies. She stops here, because to continue yields $2 + 5$, and she already has that. This child not only commutes and uses order, but she reverses the order, starting with the highest and working down.

In the exercise for number eight we see that the child has moved almost entirely at random, without being guided in any systematic fashion by logic or mathematical properties.

One discussion that comes out of this lesson arises when the child asks, "Can I have $2 + 1$ if I have $1 + 2$?" It is well to discuss this to see in what ways these statements are similar and in what ways they differ.

Children who handle the above with facility will like the more difficult problem that requires them to do the same thing with three positions. The number five worked out in this manner would look as follows:

```
        oo                    oo
     +  ooo  +         =      ooo
                              oo
     +       + ooooo   =      ooo
  oo                          oo
  ooo +      +         =      ooo
  oo                          oo
  oo  +      +     o   =      ooo
                              oo
   o + oooo +         =       ooo
  oo                          oo
  oo  +  o  +         =       ooo
                              oo
     + oooo +     o   =       ooo
                              oo
     +  o  + oooo     =       ooo
                              oo
   o +       + oooo   =       ooo
                              oo
  oo + oo  +     o    =       ooo
                              oo
  oo +  o  +    oo     =       ooo


                              oo
   o + oo + oo      =         ooo
                              oo
  oo + ooo +        =         ooo
                              oo
 ooo + oo  +        =         ooo
                              oo
 ooo +     + oo     =         ooo
                              oo
  oo +     + ooo    =         ooo
                              oo
     + oo  + ooo    =         ooo
                              oo
     + ooo + oo     =         ooo
                              oo
   o +  o  + ooo    =         ooo
                              oo
   o + ooo +  o     =         ooo
                              oo
 ooo +  o  +  o     =         ooo
```

These three-position problems are complicated enough that the child is almost forced to cast about for a more systematic, logical approach in order to ensure that he will come up with all of the possibilities. The use of permutations come into play here. This can lead to the construction of generalizations such as the following: When you have three numbers all of which are different, you get six permutations that add up to a fourth number. When you have three numbers, two of which are the same, then you get three permutations.

You can help children to see these things by putting certain restrictions on the problems you present. For example, find all the combinations that have a different number in each position and that add up to five. These would be:

+ OO + OOO = OOOOO	+ O + OOOO = OOOOO
OO + + OOO = OOOOO	+ OOOO + O = OOOOO
OOO + OO + = OOOOO	O + OOOO + = OOOOO
OOO + + OO = OOOOO	OOOO + O + = OOOOO
OO + OOO + = OOOOO	OOOO + + O = OOOOO
+ OOO + OO = OOOOO	O + + OOOO = OOOOO

Another example is to find all the cases where two of the positions have the identical number and the third position has a different number:

OO/OOO + + = OO/OOO	O + OO + OO = OO/OOO	OOO + O + O = OO/OOO
+ OO/OOO + = OO/OOO	OO + O + OO = OO/OOO	O + OOO + O = OO/OOO
+ + OO/OOO = OO/OOO	OO + OO + O = OO/OOO	O + O + OOO = OO/OOO

This can be modified further by adding another restriction, where two consecutive positions must have the same number. In this problem OO/OOO + + = OO/OOO , + + OO/OOO = OO/OOO , O + O + OOO = OO/OOO

OOO + O + O = OO/OOO , OO + OO + O = OO/OOO , and O + OO + OO = OO/OOO

would be acceptable answers, while O + OOO + O = OO/OOO would not be acceptable.

The problem can be altered to require that the three numbers add up to five, that two of them must be identical, but identical numbers may not appear side by side. These conditions make O + OOO + O = OOOOO acceptable and O + O + OOO = $\begin{smallmatrix} OO \\ OOO \end{smallmatrix}$ unacceptable.

Problems of the type given above offer many opportunities to practice addition, to think, and to gain insights into the number system and the rules of logic. Similiar problems may be set up in subtraction. An example follows.

OOOO −   = OOOO

OOOO −   OO   = OO

OOOO −   O   = OOO

OOOO − OOO = O

OOOO − OOOO =

Work can be given in addition and subtraction at the same time, helping children, with problems of the following type, to see the relationship between these two operations.

                              OOOO
OOO +   O   = OOOO   OOOO −   O   = OOO

 OO + OO   = OOOO   OOOO − OO   = OO

  O + OOO = OOOO   OOOO − OOO = O

OOOO +   = OOOO   OOOO −   = OOOO

       + OOOO = OOOO   OOOO − OOOO =

The groundwork for multiplication and division can be laid by posing problems of the following type. Using the layout below, ask the children to complete each of the statements, using the same number of tokens in each of the positions to the left of the equals sign.

                +   = OOOOOO

            +   +   = OOOOOO

  +   +   +   +   +   = OOOOOO

The finished layout, with the tokens in place, would look as follows:

$$\text{OOO} + \text{OOO} = \text{OOOOOO}$$

$$\text{OO} + \text{OO} + \text{OO} = \text{OOOOOO}$$

$$\text{O} + \text{O} + \text{O} + \text{O} + \text{O} + \text{O} = \text{OOOOOO}$$

Layouts of this kind can be worked out for any number without difficulty.

Children who successfully do the above problems can be moved to the concepts of "nine," "ten," "eleven," "twelve," etc., quite easily. Indeed, as they extend what they know of the number system, all the teacher has to add is the language of "nine," "ten," "eleven," up through "eighteen" and beyond. Eighteen is important, as the combination of the single digits of nine plus nine is the highest fact in the addition table. The children will also be able at this time to construct their own layouts and become almost entirely independent of the teacher.

Indeed, in introducing nine, ten, eleven, etc., have the children work out logically all that they can on their own. If you can tell a child who has had all of the experiences described above that $\begin{smallmatrix}\text{OOOO}\\\text{OOOO}\end{smallmatrix} + \text{O} = \begin{smallmatrix}\text{OOOO}\\\text{OOOOO}\end{smallmatrix}$ and we call $\begin{smallmatrix}\text{OOOO}\\\text{OOOOO}\end{smallmatrix}$ "nine" and the child can then observe that $9 - 1 = 8$ and $7 + 2 = 9$ and $6 + 3 = 9$ and $4 + 3 + 2 = 9$ and $7 + 1 + 1 = 9$ and $9 - 4 = 5$ and $9 - 6 = 3$, etc., then you know that you are successfully teaching the child to think, and you are equipping him to make ever more rapid progress in mathematics and other subjects. You know this because to do the above on so little new knowledge requires the application of generalizations and logical processes to the new knowledge in order to generate more knowledge. Not only is more knowledge generated, but in producing the new knowledge, the child must see to it that the new knowledge is consistent with the old knowledge. If, on the other hand, the child cannot at this time incorporate this new fact into what he has already learned, thus generating a whole new set of facts, then your teaching isn't as yet paying real dividends.

Some children will, of course, show an earlier ability than others to generate new knowledge from old; but good teaching will eventually lead all children, with the possible exception of severely brain-damaged youngsters, to produce or create or invent what is to them new knowledge. Even the so-called mentally retarded can produce new knowledge at a rate that is startling to some of their teachers, if given a chance. The key is in the teaching. Teaching is not telling, but rather it is creating situations that are pregnant with ideas with which the child can grapple and which he can solve. Teaching requires situations in which problems abound and contradictions are everywhere. The measure of good teaching is not the number of problems about which the teacher can tell her students, while offering nice clear-cut answers.

91

That may be a good measure of how much education the teacher has, but it isn't a measure of good teaching. The measure of good teaching is how many problems the children see, how many successful approaches to solving problems they have developed, and how efficiently they take the new knowledge gained from each problem that is solved and incorporate it into the knowledge they already possess in order to produce more knowledge.

LEARNING NUMERALS

We have not as yet mentioned when the writing of numerals should be introduced. Because we believe that real learning at this age comes first from manipulating the concrete environment and then from describing the environment as it is as a result of the manipulating, we have held off introducing numerals. We would like a child to have a picture in his mind of $OOO + O =$ ___ when asked, "What does three plus one equal?" This is preferable to having a picture of $3 + 1 =$ ___ in his mind. We prefer this because we believe that to answer "Four" in the first instance, the child must have, at a bare minimum, a notion of threeness and oneness and how, through addition, they equal four. To answer "Four" to $3 + 1$ may be no more than the result of Pavlov-type conditioning.

To put it another way, we prefer to deal with what three, one, and four are symbols for, and not with the symbols themselves. It is analogous to the rote recitation of the pledge to the flag done in many classrooms. We don't object to the pledge. We do object to the argument that the pledge is understood once it is memorized and recited. Those that doubt the facts in this matter need only have young children discuss the terms "pledge," "allegiance," "United States," "republic," "indivisible," etc. They will quickly find that what has been learned is verbiage. The connection between language and reality has not been made, if, indeed, there is any awareness that there is a connection.

Once children can deal adequately with the physical reality of $OOO + O$ and $OOOO - OO$ and can describe these realities with language, the numerals may be introduced. Note also that in the preceding sentences we have only pictured the reality of tokens or coins, we have not dealt with them directly. We do this of necessity and concede that pictures that represent reality are the next best thing to reality. In teaching, however, we prefer reality because it can be manipulated and observed, while pictures can only be observed.

Children may well be aware of the existence of numerals and their questions should perhaps be answered. In some cases, children will themselves begin writing these numerals and using them. They will have made the connection between physical reality, oral language, and written symbols or numerals.

A fairly systematic way of introducing the numerals is to have the children take one of their layouts and to work on problems that the teacher dictates. The children then report back to the teacher what is before them,

92

and the teacher writes the problem with its answer on the board, using numerals. The children can then write down the numerals and signs under the problem. If the children know that $3 + 4 = 7$ and have a clear notion of three-ness, fourness, fiveness, etc., the teacher can simply write any numeral the children request. The exercise to end this lesson is to ask the children to write all the numerals between zero and eight or ten in order of fewest to most and then in descending order from ten or eight to zero.

Once the children know how to write the numerals, the teacher will tend to use them more and more. He should name the numerals as he writes them, until such time as all are clear as to what numeral goes with what name.

At this point also, children should begin describing their work in writing as well as describing their work verbally. Such a statement as $7 + 5 = 12$ should be written to describe the token arrangement $7 + 5 = 12$.

In passing, let us note that a child who rather consistently writes ε for 3 or ∂ for 6 or who reads 23 as 32 or 203 as 302 should be examined for perceptual difficulties of the type we described in Chapter 3. The same child, in all probability, will be calling "tap" "pat" and "top" "pot" in reading.

MULTIPLICATION AND DIVISION

Let us turn now to the teaching of multiplication and division. It is not the case, as some believe, that the teaching of these two operations must be delayed until addition and subtraction are fully mastered. Indeed, using the Cuisenaire rods, many teachers have completely undone the traditional order of introducing mathematical concepts. We shall return to these rods later.

For those not using the rods, the multiplication operation can be taught effectively with sticks, pencils, or coffee stirrers and a few clips of a type that enable you quickly to join four or five pencils together in a group. The idea is to have the child establish three separate facts for each multiplication statement: the number of pencils in a group, the number of groups, and the number of pencils all totaled. Thus, he may have four groups with five pencils in a group, and a total of twenty pencils. He represents this as $4 \times 5 = 20$, where four stands for the number of groups, five stands for the number of pencils in each group and twenty is the total of all the pencils. Given the ability to count, the ability to clip and unclip things into groups, and the ability to set the statement down (number of groups × number of pencils in each group = the total number of pencils), the child can work out any combination concretely. More complex problems, such as $(3 \times 4) + (2 \times 5) = \underline{\quad}$, can also be worked out in this fashion.

To teach division the process is altered. If the question is, "How many fives are there in twenty?" the child first counts out twenty pencils and begins grouping them into fives until he runs out of pencils. He then counts the groups.

In introducing these two processes to children, rather than telling them how to handle the procedure, we simply demonstrate by silently clipping four pencils together and setting them down in full view, clipping four more together and placing them near the first group, clipping four more together and setting them down with the others. We count the groups by pointing as we go, saying, "Three," and writing 3 on the board. We then observe casually that "We had four in each group so that makes the problem three times four. I wonder what that equals?" We write equals next to the four and pick up all of the pencils, remove the clips, and count the pencils. Once they are counted, we write 12 next to the equal sign, count the pencils again, and regroup them. We then follow the same procedure for $4 \times 2 = 8$, $3 \times 5 = 15$, $3 \times 4 = 12$ and ask if anyone believes they can do a problem we haven't done. If not, we stop for the day. The next day we repeat one or two of the previous day's problems and introduce some others. As we do each one, we leave the results in full view. The idea, as you undoubtedly have perceived, is to have the child figure out the process or operation through observation.

One could, of course, start with division by counting out twelve pencils, quietly writing 12 on the board, and observing half out loud, "I wonder how many fours can be divided into twelve?" One would then proceed to group the pencils into fours, setting them out on the table until all the pencils were gone. We would then count the groups and write $\div 4 = 3$ next to the 12. The problem can be further sharpened by looking at the board and saying, "Twelve divided by four equals three. I guess three times four equals twelve," and proceeding to the next problem. Once the children figure out what you are doing and what it all means, they can go a long way rapidly on their own.

We shall not go into the same detail with multiplication and division as we did with addition and subtraction. We should note, however, that the same teaching strategies apply, and among other things, the children ought to be given opportunities to discover all the numbers that can be combined through multiplication to equal zero through eighty-one. They should be able to show their work using clips and pencils as well as to write all of the combinations for twenty; to give an instance: $1 \times 20 = 20$, $2 \times 10 = 20$, $4 \times 5 = 20$, $5 \times 4 = 20$, $10 \times 2 = 20$, and $20 \times 1 = 20$. They should come to recognize that addition and multiplication are commutative while subtraction and division are not. They should discover that some numbers have different characteristics than others. For example, two, three, five, seven, eleven, thirteen, and seventeen are prime numbers that can be divided equally only by the number one and by themselves, while two, four, six, eight, nine, ten, twelve, and fourteen are composite numbers and may be divided by three or more numbers. Children should observe that two is the only prime number that is also an even number. They should be able to produce the following generalizations: An even number multiplied by any other number will result in an answer that is an even number; an odd number multiplied by an odd number will yield an odd number; one multiplied by any number will yield that number; zero times any number will yield zero, etc. None of these is particularly difficult to understand if properly presented, and any standard book on elementary arithmetic will give many other statements about the number system that can be discovered by children if correctly presented.

What we have proposed above is not, in our judgment or in the judgment of an increasing number of educators, beyond the grasp of first and second graders to handle. We are confident it can be accomplished in the first grade without putting any pressure on the children that is not currently on them. That it has not been accomplished in most classrooms in the past does not disturb us. The pedagogy has been poor. Poor pedagogy doesn't make good students.

SEVEN: GETTING EFFECTIVE INSTRUCTIONAL MATERIALS

In teaching mathematics to kindergarten, first-, and second-grade youngsters, the most effective materials we have seen are the Numbers-in-Color Cuisenaire rods.[1] The Numbers-in-Color rods were introduced in this country a little over a decade ago by Caleb Gattegno. Our first introduction to them was about twelve years ago. Since then we have seen them used very effectively with remedial students, mentally handicapped students, kindergarten, and other primary-grade youngsters. It seems clear that good teachers with the Cuisenaire rods are more effective than good teachers without the Cuisenaire rods. Poor teachers, of course, are poor teachers.

[1] The Cuisenaire rods are distributed in the United States by the Cuisenaire Company of America, Inc., Mount Vernon, New York.

Because of their concreteness, the rods are particularly effective when working with young children. There are ten different sized rods. The white rod, which is the smallest, is a cube, 10 centimeters on a side. The red rod has a length of 20 centimeters and is 10 centimeters on the end dimensions. The light green rod is 30 centimeters long, the purple rod is 40 centimeters long, the yellow is 50, the dark green is 60, the black is 70, the brown is 80, the blue is 90, and the orange rod is 100 centimeters long.

Accompanying the rods (and the more you have of each, the better) is a 133-page booklet entitled *For the Teaching of Elementary Mathematics,* by Caleb Gattegno, a book that has some fascinating reading in it for the serious student of teaching.[2] Also included are *Mathematics with Numbers in Color,* a series of seven books, also by Gattegno. These last seven books are the exercises for the children and a rather comprehensive curriculum for the elementary school.

The teacher who wishes to become familiar with the rods and the curriculum need only get a set of rods and *Book I,* which is devoted to what is to be taught to beginners and in what order, and work the exercises through to the end of the book. In doing so, one learns much about mathematics, though Book I is written to be put into children's hands.

The reason the rods have been so successful is, we think, due to the fact that the child may physically do with the number system what the adult can logically do with the system. Put another way, what the adult can logically show to be the case, the child can physically show to be the case.

When these materials are used, in our judgment there is no reason why the following ideas or concepts shouldn't be developed with most youngsters during the first year of work in the kindergarten: equivalence, shorter, longer, order, complements, addition, subtraction, addition as the inverse of subtraction, odd numbers, even numbers, written signs and symbols, equations, parentheses, multiples, fractions, multiplication, division, commutativity, associativity, and a rather thorough understanding of the properties of the numbers zero to ten.

This would seem to be a lot of mathematics to teach to supposedly disadvantaged children when one considers it is much more than has traditionally been taught to supposedly advantaged children. We don't think so. Let us look at some of the things that can be accomplished with 5-year-old children and let the reader judge if it can be done. Better yet, let the reader try them out with a 5-year-old of his choice.

SUGGESTED ACTIVITIES

The rods would be arranged as depicted below if one were to build a staircase with them. We have used letters to signify the color of the rod: *w* for white, *r* for red, *g* for light green, *p* for purple, *y* for yellow, *d* for dark green, *k* for black, *n* for brown, *e* for blue, and *o* for orange.

[2] See bibliography for complete citations of books that may be used with Cuisenaire rods.

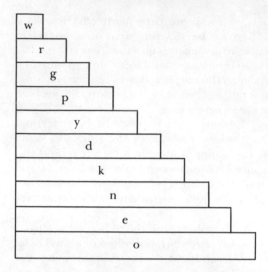

Prior to any formal lessons with the rods, the children should be given time to engage in free play with them. They will build houses, roads, and other structures and, in the process, come to be familiar with the rods and to discover some of their properties. The teacher then needs to give the children some experiences grouping the rods together according to color and according to length. Next, the children can be instructed in how to make a train, which is the rather simple process of placing the rods end to end. By placing two trains side by side, they can make a pattern.

w	r	w
p		

Above is a pattern made up of two trains. One is made up of a white rod, a red rod, and another white rod. The other is made up of one purple rod.

Once children have mastered the techniques of making trains and patterns, the world of mathematics can be opened up in earnest, as the rods hold the same relationship to each other that numbers do. Problems of an almost endless variety may be posed. Following are some examples:

1. Make a pattern for the purple rod. Make another pattern for the purple rod that is different.

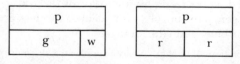

2. Make as many patterns as you can for the purple rod.

p	w	w	w	r	w	g	r
	w	w	r				
	w	r		w	g		r
	w		w	w		w	

3. Make as many patterns as you can for the yellow rod.

| y |
p	w
w	p
r	g
g	r
r	w	r
r	r	w
w	r	r
w	w	w	r
w	w	r	w
w	r	w	w
r	w	w	w
g	w	w
w	g	w
w	w	g
w	w	w	w	w

4. Make as many patterns as you can for the red rod.

| r |
| w | w |

99

5. Which pattern includes this train: white plus red plus red plus white plus red?

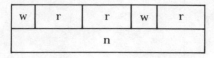

6. What rod must you put with a green rod to make a train that will pattern with the blue rod?

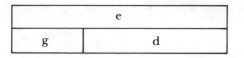

7. What rod must you put with a white rod to make a train that will pattern with the green rod?

8. Can you find two rods that will make a train that will pattern with the yellow rod?

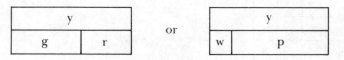

9. Can you find two rods of the same color that will make a train that will pattern with the purple rod; the brown rod; the orange rod?

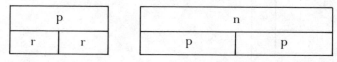

10. How many trains can you make that will pattern with the white rod; the red rod; the green rod; the purple rod; the yellow rod; the dark green rod?

100

11. Is a train made up of a red rod and a green rod longer or shorter than a black rod; than a blue rod; than a purple rod; than an orange rod; than a white rod?

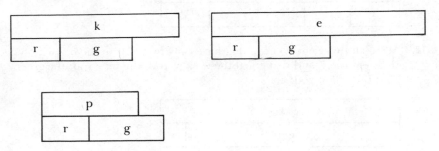

12. Is a train made up of a purple rod and a white rod longer or shorter than a train made up of two red rods; than a green and a black rod; than a white, a red, and a white rod?

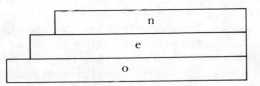

13. Arrange the rods in order so that they make a staircase.

↑ etc.

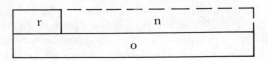

14. What rod must you add to a red rod to make an orange rod?

r	n
o	

15. Add a rod to the yellow rod so that the train will equal an orange rod.

y	y
o	

101

16. Make a train of only one color that is equal to an orange rod.

o				
r	r	r	r	r

17. Make all the trains you can that have only two rods in them, each of a different color, and that equal the orange rod; the blue rod; the green rod; the yellow rod; etc.

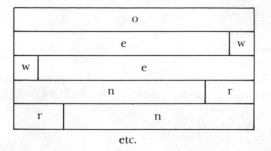

etc.

The exercises above give you some ideas as to what can be done. There are, of course, literally thousands of problems such as the ones we have offered above, all of which can be solved by the children. Once the children have demonstrated competence with the above kind of problems, they can be given letters for the different length rods, a sign for addition, the equal sign, and some appropriate language. With this equipment they can read the equivalences: $w + r = g, r + r = p, g - w = r. y - g = r$, and they can check them out with their rods. You have seen by now that from here all of the addition facts and basic subtraction facts can be worked through by the child.

Initially, children use letter symbols for the rods. Later, they learn that the rods can represent various number symbols. For example, if white equals one, then red is two, light green is three, purple is four, yellow is five, dark green is six, black is seven, brown is eight, blue is nine, and orange is ten. On the other hand, if children want to work with fractions, then brown might represent one, purple would be one-half, red would be one-fourth, and white would be one-eighth. This versatility of the rods is one factor that enables children to work so many different types of mathematical problems. Indeed, problems like those that follow are handled rather readily by young children.

To what are the following differences equivalent?

1. $5r - 2r =$

r	r	d		
r	r	r	r	r

2. $5r - 3w =$

w	w	w	k (dashed)		
r		r	r	r	r

3. $3p - 2r =$

r	r	n (dashed)	
p		p	p

4. $2k - n =$

n	d (dashed)
k	k

5. $4p - (2w + 2r) =$

w	w	r	r	o (dashed)		
p		p		p		p

6. $2k - 3g =$

g	g	g	
k		k	

7. $2(y + p) - (2w + 2g) =$

w	w	g	g	o (dashed)		
y		p		y		p

What we find appealing about the rods is that they can be used in a manner totally consistent with the pedagogical and learning principles for which we have been arguing throughout this book. Beyond this, they are a physical model of the number system that the child may manipulate to make discoveries on his own. Furthermore, a detailed curriculum has been worked out for the rods and need only be implemented by the teacher. He doesn't have to construct it himself. There are, of course, other curriculum proposals about, but we find them to be pedagogically unsound, psychologically unsound, too teacher dominated, poorly paced, or in some other way deficient.

103

In our judgment, the Cuisenaire rods, if used as recommended, will do the job in a way no other materials can. That some teachers have used them and given them up reflects more on the inadequacies of our profession than it does on the rods.

We have included this brief chapter on the Cuisenaire rods for reasons already noted and to ensure that the reader is aware of their existence. For teaching mathematics to young children they are unsurpassed, and we wouldn't be without them. We hope that those who would run a primary program for inner-city children will carefully examine the rods and the books that accompany them.

EIGHT: HELPING BEGINNING READERS SUCCEED

In this chapter we shall address ourselves to the business of teaching beginning reading. More appropriately, perhaps, we should say the business of learning to read. We advocate that reading be taught using the Words in Color method that was developed by Caleb Gattegno.[1] We urge this method in preference to other methods for several reasons. One, we believe it takes into account how children learn. This is a major point to consider. You will recall from Chapter 1 that a crucial goal of the inner-city school, as we see it, must be to teach the child to think. Most available reading programs are based

[1] Materials and explanations to the teacher are available from Educational Solutions, Inc., Post Office Box 190, Cooper Station, New York, New York 10003.

on the child's ability to memorize certain words or combinations of letters. Words in Color materials and techniques encourage children to generalize, to see relationships between sounds and symbols or between one word and another word. In short, they enable the school to work on the achievement of two basic ends at the same time: learning to read and learning to think.

Reason two is that we believe the Words in Color method has eliminated a lot of nonsense unrelated to the process of reading and the process of learning to read that abounds in many methods of teaching reading. Three, we believe it most adequately solves the problem of the irregularity of English writing. Four, we believe that if it is used correctly each child will be saved hundreds of hours, not only in the process of learning to read, but in the process of learning to spell. Five, we believe this method to be linguistically sound. Six, we have substantiated, through our own experiences, the claims made for Words in Color—it works. Seven, it is economical. Eight, we think it affords the best opportunity for developing vocabulary.

In supporting Words in Color as the means of teaching reading to children, we are not claiming it is the only way to teach reading. We are simply saying that, in our judgment, this is presently the best means available. Those who will take the time to understand how Words in Color works and who will learn how to use it and work with it will be successful in the teaching of reading and will be rewarded with remarkable growth on the part of children.

The major problem that faces the child or adult who would learn to read English is that it is a language with fifty-one sounds and twenty-six letters to represent these sounds. This is compounded to the point where these letters are arranged into over three hundred combinations to represent the fifty-one sounds. Sometimes, however, a combination of letters may represent more than one sound. For example, "ough" in "cough" is two sounds, short *o* plus *f*, while in "thought" it is one sound, short *o*. Further, sometimes one sound may be represented by a number of different combinations of letters—for example, the sound "I" in the words "I," "high," "dye," "eyes," "by," "tie," "height," "isle," "eiderdown," as well as "like."

In teaching reading, then, we have a set of sounds called "phonemes," which children know, and a set of letters and combination of letters called "graphemes," which children do not know. These two sets, as we pointed out above, are not matched sets, nor can they be put into one-to-one correspondence. There are two instances of phonemes in English where a large number of different graphemes (twenty-four in one and twenty in the other) are used to represent one phoneme. The pedagogical problem is to find a means of helping the child to seek order out of this seeming chaos.

Words in Color solves the problem by assigning a color to each phoneme. Thus, each of the underlined letters in the following words would be the same color: I, high, dye, eyes, by, tie. The "i" in "it," of course, would be another color, since it represents another sound. In Words in Color, each of the fifty-one phonemes is represented by a different coloring.

106

It is not our intention in this chapter to give a detailed account of how to teach with Words in Color. Detailed directions and explanations may be found in *Teaching Reading with Words in Color* and in the booklet called *Background and Principles*, both by Gattegno. We do feel it would be helpful, however, to give an overview, to discuss some of the techniques used to teach Words in Color, and to further suggest some other techniques that we have found helpful when teaching Words in Color to children. For the most part, we have found *Teaching Reading with Words in Color* and the materials used by the children (a set of twenty-one colored charts, three booklets in black and white that parallel the development of the charts, two sets of seven worksheets, and the book of stories) more than adequate for learning this method of reading instruction. The prospective teacher needs only to study these diligently to learn the approach.

PROCEDURES FOR INTRODUCING READING

Reading, using Words in Color, is introduced by having the teacher print the letter "a" on the board in white chalk and telling the children that this is the sign for the sound "a" (as in "pat"). The children are instructed to make the sound "a" whenever the teacher points to it or draws it on the board. They are then given opportunities to practice reading this sign. They are also given opportunities to write the sign "a."

The yellow "u" (as in "pup") is introduced next, and after the children have had some work with the yellow "u" sign the two are combined using both the pointing game and the writing game; that is, the children will read "a, u" or "u, a" or "u, a, u, a, a, u" as the teacher points to or writes these combinations. Opportunity is given to the children to read "a" and "u" in black and white by using Book I. The other short vowels are introduced in the same manner. These include "i" as in "pit," "e" as in "pet," and "o" as in "pot."

We have abbreviated six pages of detailed instruction into two very brief paragraphs. The lessons have been geared toward teaching the children a number of techniques. Among these are the ability to distinguish shapes, the knowledge that each sign requires a sound to be uttered, some understanding of how signs may be separated or linked together, and the techniques of the pointing game and the writing game.

The brown sign, "p," is introduced visually next. It is important that teachers do not introduce this letter or any other consonant as a separate entity as far as sound is concerned. The teacher should print "ap" on the board in the appropriate colors and tell the children that "The white sign followed by the brown one sounds *ap*." The teacher then asks the children what the yellow followed by the brown will sound like. The teacher is at a crucial point. Note that the teacher doesn't tell the children what "up" sounds like. The teacher *asks* what "up" sounds like. The expectation is that if the children know the sound for the sign "u" and the sound for the sign "a," and they see that the white "a" combined with the brown "p" sounds "ap," they will in effect be able to develop a principle that, if stated, would say, "If 'u' goes with 'p' as 'a' goes with 'p,' the sign 'up' must sound 'up.'" Once in a while a very bright child will, without being asked, sound "ip," "ep," and "op." If it is not volunteered, the teacher should ask what these combinations of signs would sound like. In the event the children cannot give the sound for "up," the teacher should place "a," "ap," "up," and "u" on the board and have the children sound the sign to which he points. He then points to the signs in the following order: "a," "ap," "u," "up." The children will undoubtedly handle "a," "ap," and "u" but may still not see what "up" should sound like. The teacher then tries the following: "a," "u," "a," "u," "a," "u," "ap," "up." In short, the strategy of the teacher is to bring the children to the point where they discover that the sign "u" hangs together with the sign "p" in the same way that the sign "a" hangs together with "p." The reason for these strategies is not simply that the teacher is trying to make it difficult. Nor is her objective merely to teach the children to read the word "up." If this were the case, she could have told the children that *up* is "up" in the same manner as she told them *ap* was "ap."

The teacher is striving to accomplish two other ends. First, she is trying to teach the children some strategies for thinking about how sounds and signs relate so that they have a means of untangling the huge puzzle called the English language. Second, she is trying to get them to discover how a vowel and a consonant hang together. This is a bit of knowledge that has wide application. If she can get the children to produce "up" on their own, then they can produce "ip," "ep," and "op" on their own. Then when "at" is introduced they can quickly produce "ut," "it," "et," and "ot." If the child is to progress rapidly, he needs two essential things: strategies for attacking the signs to yield English sounds, and generalizations about how the signs hang together. In our judgment, this point cannot be overemphasized.

A word that is read because the teacher has told the child what the word is, is no more than an individual word that can be read. To teach children to read the English language in this manner would be an almost hopeless task. Strategies and generalizations, on the other hand, are powerful tools the child can use to unlock more and more of the language. With each new bit of knowledge, the child can generate much more knowledge. We shall return to this point again a little later.

The children are next introduced to "pa" by the teacher, who writes "pa" on the board and gives the children the sound. The teacher then asks for the sounds of "pu," "pi," "pe," and "po." From this point on, the teacher moves to "pap," "pop," "pip," "pep," and "pup."

The sign "t" is introduced next, and then the consonant signs "s," "tt," and "ss" are also introduced. At this time, the first worksheets are introduced to the children. These are very useful for helping to develop reading vocabulary, word meanings, and writing skills.

108

THE TRANSFORMATION GAME

Following the initial work with the worksheets, the transformation game is introduced. The game has four rules: substitution of one sign for another, reversal of the order of signs in a word, insertion of a sign between other signs, and addition of a sign at either end of the word. The children are asked to transform one word into another, using the rules. "Tip" would be changed to "spat" as follows: One, we can transform "tip" to "pit" using the reversal rule. Two, we can change "pit" to "pat" by the rule of substitution. Three, we can change "pat" to "spat" by using the addition rule to add an "s." Another example is to move from "pat" to "pest." Here, we might first use the substitution rule to transform "pat" to "pet," and then use the insertion rule to put an "s" between the "e" and the "t" to form "pest."

In the worksheets and the transformation game we have fine techniques for giving the children experiences necessary for developing ways of attacking the reading problem, experiences that will enable them to construct generalizations about the language.

USING THE READING CHARTS

The teacher has also introduced the second chart by this time. The first chart showed the five vowels in their colors. The second chart shows thirty words with each of the signs in their colors. This chart is set up as follows:

pat	pit	pet	
pet	at	it	up
tap	tip	top	
pep	pup	pop	tot
as	us	is	
sat	sit	set	
stop	step	pass	
stops	steps	past	
sap	sips	test	pest

There are thirty words, nine signs, and nine colors on this chart. The "s" sign has two colors and one of the "s" colors has two signs—the single "s" and the double "ss." A number of things can be done with these charts. The pointing game can be used to form simple sentences such as "Pat is up" and "Pet it, Pat." The chief value we have found in the charts is in helping students who are having difficulty.

We have discovered in using the charts that some maneuvers are more effective than others. We keep in mind the principle that it is more beneficial, from the standpoint of learning and developing a positive self-concept in the child, for the child to find his own answers rather than to be told the answer. Therefore, with these early charts, we use the strategy that we want the child to learn for the purpose of finding his own answers. If we point to "tap" and he says "Top," rather than tell him he is wrong, we point to "top." If he again says "Top," we assume he recognizes that they both cannot be "top." We have then forced him into seeing a contradiction. To help him out of the quandary, we point to "at" and then to "pat." If the child can call these correctly, we can move back and point to "tap." If he now gets "tap" correct, we move as follows: "at," "tap," "pat," "at," "tap," "sap," "pass," "pat," "tap," in order to give him more experience with the "a" in the center of a word. As we move from one to the other, we move fairly rapidly for the same reasons as those we noted in the chapter on mathematics. Rapid accumulation of data encourages generalizations.

We have also found it useful to move about the charts in an organized fashion that may reveal insights to the children. Some of these moves include "stop," "stops," "step," "steps"; or "stop," "step," "stops," "steps"; or "pet," "pest," "pat," "past"; or "pot," "pop," "top," "tot"; or "pat," "tap," "pot," "top," "pit," "tip." There are others that are useful in helping children, but we leave them for the serious reader to discover. The general rule we use when working with children on the charts is to move about the chart until an error is made, to point to the word that, if called correctly, will point up to the child that he has erred, to then move to another word that will give him some insight into what the correct response ought to be. The best way to do this is to move to words you know the child knows. If he has called "pep" "pip," it is not sufficient to move only to "pit" so that he sees he has made an error. This is a necessary move because he can then see that the sound in the middle of "pit" is not the one in the middle of "pep" as he had first thought, but it doesn't give him a clue as to what the "e" sound is — only what it isn't. You also need to point to a word with the "e" in it in order for the child to solve the problem. Sometimes you can go directly to "pet" when "pep" has been called "pop" or "pip" and then go back to "pep" and get the correct response. The first strategy is the better of the two, however. The second strategy still leaves something unanswered — namely, if "pep" is "pep" and not "pip," what is the sign for "i"?

Once you find the child making an error that is due to causes other than carelessness, then you need to work at some length on the problem. If the child makes a couple of errors on the blue "e," don't spend the next ten minutes playing with the "i" and the "o." Work on the "e." It is even useful to make flashcards or special charts, using words that contain the troublesome sign. You should include on the special chart words that are not on the chart with which you are currently working. We have not made an exhaustive study but have found twenty-four words that can be made up with the signs and phonemes used on Chart 2 that are not included on the chart. Using the additional signs of "m" and "n," which appear on Chart 3, we have found another fifty words without any difficulty. By the way, when you can introduce these words in black and white and have the children read them in an instant, you can be confident that you must be doing something right.

We should like to say a word about pace at this point. Many teachers make the mistake of staying with a chart until the child can "read" every word. Our own experience tells us that it is a good idea to move on to the next chart before this time. If the child can handle most of the words excepting those that start with "t," and he still does not see the solution, despite your having given some additional attention to these "t" words, don't belabor the point. Move on. To stop is to increase the child's frustrations and your own. Furthermore, you restrict the data. If you move on to the next chart, the same problem is there in "tim," "tom," and a number of other words. In addition, the child is learning many other things. He is progressing, and as long as he sees progress he will feel kindly toward himself and the act of reading. This will help to keep him plugging away at the problem.

We should like to illustrate this point with an experience we had with a 14-year-old nonreader who had a problem common to many youngsters who spent their early years in the South. This boy learned the sounds for the signs "a," "o," "u," rather readily. He had, however, a great deal of difficulty distinguishing "i" and "e." He told us in the fourth hour of instruction that he couldn't hear any difference. Despite all of the work on Charts 1 and 2 and despite the construction of another chart that had two columns of words, he couldn't hear the difference. The new chart looked, briefly, as follows:

pet	pit
pep	pip
set	sit

All the "e's" were in blue, all the "i's" were pink. The instructor read the lists up and down and back and forth, and the boy still said he couldn't hear the difference.

In the sixth hour of instruction we were working with Chart 3 and this boy read "not" and "nut" correctly, and we pointed to "net." He sounded "net" correctly, his face lit up, and he said, "I can spell nit," which he did. He then correctly read "ten," "tent," "sent," "in," and "met" on Chart 3. He moved over to Chart 2 and read all of the words correctly. Needless to say, he was quite excited.

One point to be made here is that if you can keep the child succeeding, he will keep trying. This boy may not have been hearing a difference between "i" and "e," but he was hearing other differences and learning the sounds for other signs. He was becoming aware that there was a difference between "i" and "e," even if he couldn't hear it. He was quietly wrestling with the problem and becoming confident, as he solved other problems, that he would eventually solve this one. Which, of course, he did.

The second point to be made here is that, once the boy saw the difference between "net" and "nit" and could sound them out, he knew all he needed to know to read all of Charts 1 and 2. The knowledge immediately transferred back over his past experience. In one shot, so to speak, he was able to undo all previous mistakes. He now had the key to "tip," "sit," "set," "it," "pep," "pit," "is," "sips," "pet," "pest," "tent," "tim" etc. If we had stayed with the problem back in the beginning and solved it in the sixth hour, all he would have known was the sounds for "a," "e," "i," "o," and "u." The rule is: Don't panic when the child fails to solve a particular problem. Move on to other matters. The problem in question will come up again and again in all sorts of places. Keep the child learning and in one of these places a solution will be seen.

To illustrate this point with an example from mathematics, let us note that it is shortsighted to try to teach the commutative property of addition with the single instance of $2 + 3 = 3 + 2$, when there are an infinite number of instances of this property. We believe the teacher's attitude ought to be, "Okay, you don't see anything here. Fine, we'll be here tomorrow and the next day. You'll see it soon. You're too smart not to see it. I didn't see it until I became a teacher, and I'm not getting excited if you don't see it until later. You saw a lot of things today, and if you keep looking you'll see something here." It is not necessary to verbalize all this, but let it guide you just the same.

Patience is a virtue in teaching. The "e" and the "i" sound make up 4 percent of the sounds in English. Six or seven hours isn't too long a time to get the distinction.

OTHER USEFUL PROCEDURES

There are several other techniques we have found beneficial while working with children and Words in Color. One, mentioned in an earlier chapter, that we have found to be useful is the "You're-the-Teacher" technique. Sometimes, as a change of pace and as a means of taking the pressure off the child, this game helps. We have played it by pointing to words the child names. We have also played it by printing the words the child requests. The best way, We feel, is to structure the game so that it tends to force the child eventually to face the signs and sounds with which he is having trouble, while at the same time enabling him to avoid the problem, for the time being at least. If we have a child who has spent some time on Chart 2 and handles the "p" and the "t" reasonably well but is still having a little difficulty with a couple of the vowels, we will structure the game in the following manner. We ask the child if he wants us to write "pat," "pet," "pit," "pot," or "put" on the board. Once he tells us which word he wants, we write it and it is his job to tell us if we are right or wrong. The strategies to be used in this game are the same as when playing the game in mathematics.

Another technique involves permitting the child to think about his own problem. In working with Words in Color, or at any other time when a teacher is working with a group of children, the teacher is presenting data with which the children must deal, and he is structuring data in a manner he hopes will bring children to see a particular relationship. He probably has organized the data in a particular way to foster a particular generalization that he knows is important for the children to discover. It is, however, impossible to organize data in such a manner that only one generalization may be drawn. The consequence of this is that a child here or there in the group may see some connection other than the one the teacher is after. If children have been encouraged to think, to reflect, and to analyze, they will often do just that. But thinking, reflecting, and analyzing are solitary activities, and the child must withdraw into himself and carry on a dialogue with himself if he is to come to any conclusions. He may, therefore, look out the window. His mind does indeed wander. Many teachers interrupt this dialogue, or daydreaming, and try to bring the child back to the problem the teacher is interested in having the group solve. This is, in our judgment, a mistake. If our objective is to get children to think and reflect, let us not stop it when it starts. From the standpoint of teaching children to think, the perfect lesson would be one in which every child has discovered something in the data that has raised a problem that he sees as significant and worth his attention. Further, he not only sees what he believes to be a significant problem, but he is actively seeking a solution by constructing and testing hypotheses that may lead to a solution. If each child takes such a problem home with him each night—one he has spotted on his own—then learning of a significant nature will be inevitable.

"But," some will object," how do you know that the child has a problem on which he is working?" Maybe he is bored or lazy or tired or just "goofing off." Our response is that if he is tired, let him rest. If he is lazy, we suggest he be given a metabolism test by a competent physician. If he is bored or goofing off, something is wrong with the teaching. The teacher has a problem, and the child is indicating it. Bored children in a classroom are indicative of poor teachers in the classroom. The teacher should analyze and reflect upon the data in the classroom to see if he can solve his problem.

Some may observe that the reason for the child's lack of involvement may not be any of those suggested above. The child might be afraid of the work. He may not be able to make head nor tail of the data and, therefore, is running away. Again, it is the teacher's problem. Don't force the child to come back to the lesson. If he is that afraid of it, he undoubtedly will fail and then what have we gained? Restructure the lesson so that the child can handle it and gain from it. Too much anxiety inhibits learning. If a child has so much anxiety that he cannot face the data in front of him, let him off the hook.

Let us make another observation on children who "tune out" on lessons. Many a child—more, we suspect, than most realize—who is apparently tuned out, isn't. He may look as though he isn't paying attention, and he may, for reasons of his own, keep the act up for several days, but eventually he decides to play the game like the others, and you are surprised to find that he learned a great deal by not paying attention. We know of one instance where a "disadvantaged low-IQ youngster" was observed by two college seniors while the teacher introduced some new material in a subject area (linguistics) about which the child knew nothing. The seniors reported that this child heard "absolutely nothing for the four days." On the fifth and last day of the unit, the boy demonstrated that he could handle any of the problems placed before the group, and the two girls concluded that he was among the top three students in the class. Other instances of this phenomenon are reported by other observers. We're not sure of the reason. Perhaps, it is simply that children, like adults, have days when they don't feel like talking and answering questions. They tend to retire and quietly watch the world go by. This doesn't mean the brain in their heads has stopped functioning or that they are not observing the passing scene and learning from it. There is no way in the world short of killing them that you can stop children from learning. The trick is to put into the classroom things that will enable them to learn something of value.

In closing this chapter, we should like to make something perfectly clear. We have not attempted a full description of the Words in Color method. It would be foolish to do so when the task has already been superbly done by Dr. Caleb Gattegno and his capable associate, Dr. Dee Hinman. We do not even feel we have done a job that is sufficiently adequate to enable professionals in the reading field to pass judgment on the program. We have merely attempted a brief description in order to report some techniques that we have found beneficial when working with Words in Color. These techniques are intended to supplement the techniques that are described in the teacher's materials that accompany the Words in Color program. Needless to say, we feel it is an outstanding program and a tremendous contribution to the reading field. Why so many reading experts have chosen to ignore it is best answered by the experts. We don't expect much of an answer.

NINE: INDIVIDUALIZING READING INSTRUCTION

We indicated earlier that reading, as we see it, is the act of matching the sound system to the written system. To learn to read, we argued, is to learn to move from the written system to the sound system. Once this has been learned, the child is in a position to learn from what he reads. He can now receive the communications of others through the written word. His world is expanded in that he can listen to many more people as a reader than as a nonreader. He has become freer.

This chapter deals primarily with the reading curriculum for the child who can read, in that he can move from the written system to the sound system. Before dealing with this question, however, we need to stop for a moment and deal with the child who has failed to learn how to read by the time he reaches the second grade.

Children may fail to learn to read in the first grade for a number of reasons. Long illnesses, sustained emotional crisis in the home, severe brain damage, visual difficulties, and hearing difficulties are a few of the possible contributing factors. The school cannot respond in any meaningful way to some of these factors. Others, the school will have worked to solve or mitigate.

As the year starts, a school that has been reasonably successful in implementing our proposals will face four kinds of second-grade reading groups. The first group will be those youngsters who have successfully learned to decode the written language and who are ready to profit from a diet of wide reading. The second group will contain those youngsters who made considerable progress toward the end of the first year and need only time to complete the Words in Color program. The third group will be students who have transferred into the school and have failed to learn to read because of poor instruction. The fourth group will be made up of those youngsters who, despite all efforts, still cannot read.

We shall deal with the first group later in the chapter. The solution for the second group is, of course, to continue the program during reading period. A program during the summer would be another way to respond to this group.

The third group should be given the Words in Color program during the reading period. They should follow the program from the beginning through to its completion, working with a paraprofessional. They simply work with the paraprofessional while the other children carry out their reading activities.

WORKING WITH THE NONREADERS

The fourth group of children is a more difficult problem and, we should note, may include some students who have transferred in from other schools. It is with these youngsters that education becomes most like a science. We have applied all the knowledge, techniques, and skill at our disposal and still the child doesn't read. Furthermore, we know that if we don't succeed in teaching him to read soon, he will be under a tremendous handicap in his other school work in the future. At this point, a clinical approach is probably as good as any. Gather all the data you can on the child. Get a complete medical checkup and a complete psychological work-up. When all the data are gathered and the reports are in from all quarters, suggestions as to how to proceed will undoubtedly be forthcoming.

Hearing and visual problems should have been discovered earlier. Some difficulties, such as brain damage, however, are more difficult for teachers to discern. Some of these youngsters may fall into one of several categories of brain damage or other disability that makes it virtually impossible for the school to deal with them in that they need special expertise. Arrangements should be made for these children to be placed in special schools or to receive special help by professionals trained to handle the child's problem. The point we wish to make is that the role of the individual teacher is not to be all things to all children. Teaching is a difficult enough enterprise without requiring teachers to be medical or psychological experts. On the other hand, the school is obligated to recognize that it has failed, that the failure may be due to some disability, that the disability may be discernible to experts from other fields, and that once identified the child has a right to be placed where he can be aided in his struggle to learn about the world.

It may well be that in some instances no medical reason can be found for the child's failure to learn. He is found to be of sound body and mind. The failure, then, must be viewed as the school's failure. This may not be the case, but one must presume that it is. That is to say, the failure may be a physical or mental one that the experts didn't detect. The school, however, has no expertise by which it can second-guess the experts whom it calls upon for help in these matters, other than to get another set of experts, who may agree with the first set. The school must face the fact that they have a child with whom they have so far failed and that no explanation for the failure is available.

In these cases, we make two observations and one or two recommendations. Observation one is that if you study the child's case history it will show that the child did learn. He can read some words, he has some concepts of number, he can speak, etc. In short, he has learned something, from which you can conclude that there are conditions under which he learns. Observation two is that you have a golden opportunity here to learn more about your theory of instruction. What we have proposed as a curriculum and as a way to teach will, by no means, be the last words on the subject. We have in these last two pages anticipated its possible inadequacy—its failure, if you will. It is the child who fails and whose failure cannot be explained by the theory that gives one the opportunity to reexamine the theory, for this child presents the anomaly. If every care has been taken to honestly apply the pedagogy proposed and the child fails even though he has all of the abilities the pedagogy requires, then the opportunity for improving the pedagogy is at hand.

Given the above, it is the leader who should take over the instruction of these children. If not the leader, it should be a supervisor or a college education professor. It should be someone whose major concern is the improvement of pedagogical theory. But alas, few who claim to be interested in theory will work with children.

The second alternative is to take a highly intelligent teacher who has some appreciation of the theory, who has an abundance of patience, and who believes every child can and will learn. The administration should then give this teacher everything he asks for and get out of the way, letting the teacher come to grips with the problem. This is the best suggestion we can make until schools realize that they need scholars in residence to study anomalies. Our suggestion won't do a thing for improving theory, but it may do something for one or two children. Refinement of a theory might have helped thousands more.

117

INDIVIDUALIZING THE PROGRAM
FOR SUCCESSFUL READERS

Let us now return to our first group of children who have learned to decode and who are ready to gain knowledge from the act of reading. The child who has had a successful experience in learning to read wants to read. It is not unusual for children to read more than two hundred books in the first grade. Our view is that the second-grade program should enable the children to read and read and read. Let them read everything and anything they wish. If they develop an interest in one of the uncommon learning centers, let them pursue it. If they are hopped up on a hobby, let them read. Whatever the interest, let them read. The school's role is to make the materials available to enable the child to pursue the interest, to support the child in his role of reader, and to assist him in profiting from his reading. Below, we shall make a few suggestions of specific activities that might be incorporated into the curriculum, but by and large the guiding proposition should be to let the children read.

The success of such a reading program rests with the library. A successful school library in an inner-city school should be open all hours of the day and a good part of the evening. Children from crowded inner-city homes need a place to read that is quiet and relaxing.

A successful school library will also be built around the interests the children have and are likely to develop. The library ought to contain a wide range of books that relate to the centers in the school. The uncommon learning centers will create an interest, the library will feed that interest — will help to educate the child — and the child will, in turn, carry the knowledge back to the center and make it a more vital and exciting center. In the process, children will learn something of the value of reading.

For the same reasons, the library ought to have materials that describe, and are related to, the places the children are likely to visit on trips. The library ought to relate to television. If Star Trek is big on television, the library ought to be responsive and offer a wide variety of books on space. The library, in brief, must touch those aspects of reality that the child touches. Money is a variable that affects libraries. The PTA members would do well to: one, insist on an outstanding library; two, insist that it be adequately staffed; three, insist that it be kept open; four, raise additional funds to support it; and five, use it for their own pleasure. Parents who read will learn, but more important for our purposes, their children will read.

What holds for parents holds for teachers when it comes to reading. The child who has read a book and finds a teacher who has also read the book comes to believe that reading the book was of value, and the act of having read the same book brings that child and that teacher closer together. They have a common experience that they can discuss. They have, in the author of that book, a common "acquaintance" that neither has met but about whom each can wonder.

118

The teacher who cares will spend a half hour each day getting to know the library. The knowledge he gains comes into play time and time again in dealing with children, and as the knowledge is displayed, the children come to see the many values in reading. Teachers can, if they know the books the children are reading, give additional insights to the children by the comments they make about a book and its author and by the questions they ask of the child about the book. Good books are value-laden. Good books relate to people and living. Teachers who know the books the children are reading can reveal these facts to children through their comments and questions.

The teacher can also encourage children to reread some books. Rereading a book after it has been discussed generally provides the reader with new insights. Aspects of the story that were not noted in the first reading add new depth to the story, and familiarity with the story can heighten enjoyment.

We also feel that a teacher can help children to be more sophisticated readers through an oral reading program in which the teacher reads to the class for short periods of time. Oral reading is becoming a lost art, but skillful oral reading, we believe, makes for better listeners and for better readers. It also provides an opportunity to introduce children to poetry and literature that they cannot yet read for themselves. Too often, reading aloud to children terminates in the kindergarten. An uncommon learning center for oral reading and story telling would not be amiss in our judgment.

The teacher should also introduce the children to the dictionary and ask them to discover its organization and its purposes. The key word here is "discover." Don't tell them. Give them the dictionary and say, "Your problem is to find out what this book is, what it can be used for, and what is the most effective way of using it. Look at it carefully and then try to describe it." This is also the way to introduce children to the library. Tell them, "This is a library. Find out all you can about this library. Then try to describe it for others." They will have had previous practice in describing reality with such games as "Describe Me" (see Chapter 10), and therefore will have learned a means of attacking the problem. In each case you, in effect, ask the children to describe the concrete reality before them. This procedure is much more effective than if you tell them about dictionaries and libraries. If telling was the most effective way of teaching, we would tell the children about numbers and reading and language. If telling about numbers won't work, why should telling about dictionaries and libraries work? Be consistent. Give the child the data, pose the problem, and let him go. He may discover some things about libraries and dictionaries that you didn't know.

This does not imply that the teacher should not tell the children anything about the dictionary or library. On the contrary, if a child asks a question about a library practice that is based on an arbitrary decision, the teacher should provide the information. If a child wants to test out an idea he has about the function or organization of the library, the teacher should give him feedback as to the accuracy of his idea. If a child has noted a general trend of organization, the teacher may need to help him structure the data so that he can discover the more specific aspects of organization.

For example, a child may note that some books are labeled with letters and other books are labeled with numbers. He might report this to the teacher and ask, "Does that mean there are two different kinds of books?" The teacher would say, "Yes, your idea is right." Here, the teacher is providing feedback for the child's testing of an idea. The teacher then would suggest that the child look carefully at three or four lettered books and three or four numbered books. "See if you can find any differences between the two kinds of books." Here, the teacher is helping the child to structure the data for further analysis.

After comparing the two sets of books, the child may say, "These books with letters on them are all storybooks. But the ones with numbers on them don't have stories. They tell about how to do things and stuff like that. There are lots of different numbers. Do they stand for something special?" The teacher could then indicate the large categories of the Dewey decimal system, which is, after all, an arbitrary organization of information.

The teacher should be careful not to answer an all-encompassing question such as, "What's a dictionary for?" This would end the child's search in short order. However, children can share and compare their observations and descriptions with each other. This kind of pooling of information will speed the discovery process and help children learn some of the techniques of cooperative inquiry.

We are not enthusiastic about book reports for second graders, nor are we enthusiastic about their use in high school or in college. We would, however, like to see communication in the classroom relating to books. This communication can take place at any time, and part of the time set aside for reading may, on occasion, be given over to the children for recommending to their classmates books they have read. These recommendations should be brief, and what goes into them and how they are to be reported should be worked out by the children. A space on the bulletin board might be set aside where children can write book recommendations for their classmates. These recommendations can be more detailed if the children so desire it.

Book jackets should be displayed about the room as suggestions, and the teacher who knows her library will be able to make additional suggestions, as will the librarian. Children should also be encouraged to sample books, to take them off the shelf, to read a few pages, and then to decide if they wish to read the book or not. Children should be encouraged to take several books out at a time. Fifty or sixty library books ought to be out in each classroom, and these should be exchanged at the time when they are not being given steady use. Multiple copies of popular books ought to be on hand.

During the reading period, the teacher should not hesitate to sit at his desk and read a book. Nor should he hesitate to say that he felt a book wasn't too good if he is asked and if he feels the book is a poor one. The teacher must be prepared to offer judgments on books and, most important, to make his criteria for judging books explicit. The old saw that each and every book is a thing to be treasured is nonsense. We don't advocate book burning, but we do advocate not reading books that have little to offer except royalties for their authors. A teacher who observes to a child that he liked a book because it made him think, or it brought a subject alive, or it left him sad, or it was beautifully written suggests to the child some of the things books can do and sends the child to a book asking himself: "Does this book make me think? What is it that makes this a beautifully written book? What can I expect from a book and its author?" These are important questions, not easily answered. The teacher can, however, move the child toward an awareness of these questions and others, and in so doing, begin the development of literary taste and literary criticism. It is as important for teachers of second graders as it is for the college teacher of literature to know something of literary criticism. No formal instruction of literary criticism is recommended, but children ought to begin to realize that there are books, and then again there are books.

During the reading period, discussions should be held with individual children about books in general, and the children should draw on their own reading experiences to deal with these discussions. The teacher should ask the child about the book the child is currently reading. Some of these questions should be open ended, and some should be specific. The child should be given an opportunity to read aloud to the teacher. The discussion should also direct itself to what reading plans the child has for the future. Through talking with the child, through listening to him read, and through questioning him about his reading, the teacher will become aware of the child's weaknesses as a reader.

The child may miss important detail, or see the detail and miss the larger point. The young reader may not effectively use context clues to get meaning, or he may give literal interpretations when a figurative interpretation is required. He may have other weaknesses. The teacher should note to himself each child's weakness and work with the child on his weakness.

Beyond working with each child, the teacher should bring together into small groups those children who have a particular weakness and work with them as a group. The idea is to construct a lesson or lessons for all children who do not utilize context clues. Those children who do use context clues should be left to go about the business of reading. Groups in this reading program, then, center around problems and remain only as long as the problem remains. Occasionally, a problem will be seen on which the whole group needs work. Then and only then will there be a lesson in which the whole group participates.

In order to keep track of weaknesses that particular children have, the teacher will need to have records of reading progress that are not time-consuming to keep and that are easy to interpret. There are many simple systems that have been devised for this purpose, and descriptions of them are available in the literature on individualized reading programs.[1]

[1]See bibliography for a sample list of the available literature.

As outlined above, the major thrust of the second-grade reading program is to develop increased independence in reading skills and to increase children's desire to read. This kind of reading program permits maximum interaction with the less formal aspects of the curriculum, such as the field trips, uncommon learning centers, and scholarship days.

TEN: JUSTIFYING CLASSROOM CONVERSATION

Language learning is often thought of as being very complex, and there is no question that it is perhaps hard to understand how we learn our language. Nevertheless, children do learn to speak their native tongues at an early age. Children apparently learn language in part through imitation and in part through an intuitive reasoning that they use to associate speech and action. Also involved in the process of learning language are other speakers of the language whom the child uses in order to get feedback or to reinforce the speech patterns he is testing.

The intonation and stress patterns are learned long before words are enunciated. In the babbling of babes we can hear the intonation of a statement-type utterance or a question that is being asked. We may not, as listeners, know *what* question is being asked, but we are confident one is being asked; and we soon learn, as parents, that we are expected to answer. The child listens and imitates. What thought he is expressing is hard to know. The nouns and verbs are there, as well as some other structures, but meaning eludes us.

Children, however, are observant, and eventually they see correlations between two sets of phenomena. The first set is speech. The second set is reality. A child trips over a rug and mother says, "My girl tripped over the rug." The child spills milk and mother says, "Oh, you have spilled milk on my rug." The child's mother says to the child's older brother, "Please pick up your baseball cards from the living-room rug." The older brother is then seen picking his cards up from the rug. The common denominator in each of these events is the rug. The common denominator in each bit of speech is the sound "rug." The child puts two and two together and points to the rug and says, "Rug." Mother says, "Yes," and makes a big fuss over her child, and the word "rug" is learned. Later, the child may trip over a toy and go crying to her mother who says, "Did my baby trip over the nasty old toy?" We can only guess, but our thinking is that the child notes that she fell twice, and each time her mother used the word "trip." The four events of tripping over the rug, tripping over the toy, and mother using the term "trip" on each occasion leads the child to associate the word "trip" with the action that took place on each occasion.

It is essentially by this intuitive, associational process that the child learns the bulk of the vocabulary he is to learn. Last week at a neighbor's house, we were sharing a roll of individually wrapped candies with our 4 1/2-year-old, when the hostess set a large ashtray down in front of us and commented, "You can dispose of your wrappers in this." As we unwrapped each candy, we put the wrapper in the ashtray, asking as we did so, "Where shall I dispose of my wrapper?" Each time the child pointed to the ashtray. We then asked her where she would dispose of her wrappers? Each time she pointed to the ashtray and was told, "Yes, put the wrapper in the ashtray." Later that evening she asked if she should "dispose of" her ice-cream wrapper in the garbage pail.

To give another example, we recently had some very high winds that were referred to as a "hurricane." On television that evening, the first hurricane of the season was reported. All winds are now referred to as "hurricanes."

Children learn other language constructions in this same intuitive manner. We sometimes are amused by the child who buys a toy and observes that, "It costed me ten cents." What the child has done, however, is rather insightful. He has observed that we add "ed" to certain words when we wish to place an event in the past. Happily, children are not rigorous logicians and accept our correction that "cost," not "costed," is the correct usage.

One further observation on the learning of language: It has often been said children should attend to one thing at a time, and further, that children have short attention spans. Our observations of children seem to show that each of these statements is false. We once observed a 3-year-old who swung back and forth on a swing for forty uninterrupted minutes while talking out loud unceasingly. The child, among other things, was, we submit, practicing language.

Children, then, learn the language by hearing it, by making connections between it and the real world, by seeking out these connections and testing them, and by practicing speech. The sounds of the language, the words of the language, the syntactical structures of the language, the meanings of the language are all learned in this manner. Given the physical abilities of the senses and some intelligence as a starting point, all children learn to speak the language they hear.

LANGUAGE LEARNING IN THE SCHOOL

Where many schools abort language learning is by making the written word the heart of the language arts program. Where many teachers stunt language growth is by talking down to children through the selection of words "the children will understand," through talking the "children's language." This is, we submit, poor procedure. In the first place, language is oral, not written. In the second place, English is a redundant language. One needs to hear little of a conversation to know all of what is being said.

A college professor we know did a week of arithmetic demonstration lessons in a disadvantaged second grade. He introduced his first lesson by stating that he wished to play an intellectual game with the children. The children didn't say anything, and he proceeded to teach his lesson. At the end of the lesson, the substitute teacher who had the class for the day reprimanded the professor for using language the children didn't understand. The professor, as he related the story, stated that he had never thought much about his language, and he had thought less about children. Knowing little about children, however, he decided to proceed as he had planned, particularly as his lesson went well. He did decide on a test, however, and each day he started his lesson by asking if the children would like to play another intellectual game. On the last day of his visits, he asked the children what an "intellectual game" was. His comment later was, "You know, those kids not only identified all the variables I saw in intellectual games but two other variables of which I'd never thought. I don't see where they are disadvantaged."

We infer from all of the above some guidelines for running first grades that will aid language development in children. One, adults working with children should never hesitate to speak the language they ordinarily speak. In fact, saying "Dispose of your paper in the waste basket" is preferred to saying "Throw your paper in the waste basket" because the children have all learned what "throw" means in this context and thus can learn little from its being used again. If adults working with children have a limited vocabulary, they should make an effort to expand their own vocabularies. Two, adults should make use of long sentences. Three, opportunities for carrying out small-group discussions should not be overlooked. Walking five children to another part of the building is a good time to carry on discussions that introduce ideas and words, and an opportunity is offered for children to practice language. Eating lunch with children is another opportunity; so is riding on the bus while taking a field trip. Standing in line at dismissal is another opportunity. Adults should seek out every opportunity to engage children in conversation. It is at such moments that the learning of language takes place. Four, opportunities should be given for children to talk with each other. A quiet room may please parents and the principal, but it doesn't aid language learning.

The above are some general conditions necessary for fostering continued language development on the part of children. We should now like to look at some specific activities that we feel are essential to the language development of children. These activities focus on three areas of language development: increasing children's vocabularies; increasing children's active use of oral communication; increasing children's awareness of the structure of English and encouraging them to make use of a greater variety of structural patterns.

INCREASING CHILDREN'S VOCABULARIES

The important thing to remember in planning activities to increase vocabulary is that words represent concepts. This does not necessarily mean that a child who lacks words is also lacking in concepts, but it does mean that learning a new word is basically like learning a new concept. For this reason, the principles developed in studies of concept learning are applicable to the learning of vocabulary.

Two basic principles guided the planning of the activities that follow. First, attainment of a concept requires that the learner be given several examples of things that represent that concept, as well as several examples of things that do *not* represent that concept. In the "normal" course of events, a child learning the word "dog" first hears the word applied to one particular animal, perhaps a collie. The child, however, probably generalizes this word to a large number of animals, so that cats, pigs, or even horses may be called "dog." Gradually, he learns to restrict the word "dog" and no longer applies it to cats, pigs, or horses. He also learns to extend the word "dog" to cover Chihuahuas, cocker spaniels, and Great Danes. This is a slow process, because the examples and non-examples of the word "dog" are usually met by chance. In the classroom, however, the learning process can be speeded up by presenting examples and non-examples of a word or concept together in one lesson.

Second, to increase the accuracy and speed of understanding, words or concepts should be introduced in relation to concrete experiences. A picture is not a concrete experience, it is a representation of the concrete. Pictures are useful to help children *recall* their experiences with the real thing, for instance a cow; but, if the children have never had any experience with a real cow, then pictures of cows are very apt to cause the child to develop misconceptions. This is particularly true for children who come to school without much prior exposure to picture books or magazines.

With these two principles in mind, the teacher can plan many types of activities to help increase children's vocabulary. Of course, it is expected that the teacher has some awareness of what words the children do know or do not know. He can gain this awareness by listening to children's conversations or by deliberately introducing various objects into the classroom.

A good game to play to give the teacher this type of information is "Describe Me." One object or a series of objects can be used, depending on the time available and the children's interest. Children are shown the object and are encouraged to handle it. They are then asked to describe the object. The idea of the game is to see how many different kinds of things they can notice and say about the object. The class, or a small group, works cooperatively at this, as in a brain-storming session, and one idea tends to suggest another. When introducing this game to children, the teacher can help to indicate possible kinds of descriptions by adding her own statements periodically to those of the children. A basketball might provoke the following sample of comments:

CHILD: It's a ball.
CHILD: It's big.
CHILD: It's brown.

Long pause

TEACHER: It's not red.
CHILD: It's not blue.
CHILD: It's not green.
CHILD: It's not yellow.

Long pause

TEACHER: I can roll it on the floor.
CHILD: I can throw it.
CHILD: I can catch it.

Long pause

TEACHER: It's not square.

Long pause

The teacher must analyze these comments in terms of what is said and, more importantly, in terms of what is not said. This sample of descriptions suggests to the teacher that knowledge of words referring to colors and shapes may be somewhat limited. "Bounce" may not be a familiar word, and children may not know names of various types of balls, such as football," "baseball," "golf ball." This suggests terms that can be introduced to children at a later date.

The teacher needs to make some decisions about which words are most crucial for children to know. Those that she deems most important would be handled in a lesson. Those that are less important could be introduced in a more informal manner. Thus, during the above exchange, the teacher might

127

decide that "bounce" was not a word worthy of a separate lesson. In this case, she would say, "I can bounce the ball," and she would bounce the ball to several children in turn to demonstrate briefly the meaning of the word "bounce."

As mentioned earlier, the teacher needs to make constant use of opportunities to use unfamiliar words in meaningful settings so that the children have a chance to increase their vocabulary through informal learning as well as through formal learning.

As children learn to play the game, "Describe Me," new possibilities for descriptions can be introduced by the teacher, such as changing the position of the object in space in order to say, "It's on the table," or, "It's under the desk," or, "It's behind my back." Depending on what the teacher wants to know, such variations are almost limitless.

This game has the advantage of working two ways. The teacher is getting information about the children, and at the same time the children are learning. A word that is familiar to one child is heard by others and related to a concrete object. Careful observation of various aspects of objects is encouraged by the desire to get lots of descriptions. All of this occurs in a nonthreatening situation. No child is put on the spot to give an answer that will then be labeled "right" or "wrong."

A variation of "Describe Me" is to give children three objects to observe and handle. They then close their eyes and one of the objects is hidden. When the children open their eyes, they must describe the missing object, mentioning all the things they can recall about it.

Children's responses in these games may be recorded on a tape recorder for later playback and analysis by the teacher. Later in the year, when reading ability has been developed, the teacher can record responses on a chart for children to read back to themselves, if they so desire. Such a written record will give children some obvious proof of their increasing ability to describe things, as their lists grow longer and longer.

Once the teacher decides what words need to be learned, he can plan lessons around a particular word. He might, for example, assemble the following items: two red apples, two yellow apples, two green apples, two peaches, two oranges, two bananas, two tomatoes, a red rubber ball, and a red balloon. These would be displayed in two groups. One group would include all the apples. The other group would include all the other items. Children would be told, "These are apples, and these things are not apples." They would be asked to look at and handle both groups of things, then various items would be considered in turn.

"This is an apple. How is it like the other apples? How is it different from the other apples?"

"This is not an apple. It's a banana. How is it different from the apples? How is it like the apples?"

"This isn't an apple. It's a tomato. How is it different from the apples? How is it like the apples?"

128

After the objects have been discussed, they can be investigated further. One of the apples can be peeled, one cut in half, and one cored and sliced. One each of the peaches, oranges, bananas, and tomatoes can also be cut in half and half might be peeled. Again children can discuss the similarities and differences among the various items.

Finally, two paper plates (previously prepared) can be provided for each child. On one plate would be apple slices, on the other plate would be slices of peach, orange, banana, and tomato. As the children eat these, the teacher would point out once again that one plate has apples, while the other has things that are not apples. The flavors and textures can be compared; e.g., "Which things make a noise when you bite into them? Which do not? Which things are very juicy? Which aren't?"

At this point, the teacher can return to the remaining original items, which were not cut into pieces, and ask the children to identify each item in turn as either "an apple" or "not an apple." The "defining characteristics" of apples that have been mentioned can be reviewed by children and teacher together: "You eat them." "They are sort of round." "They can be red or yellow or green on the outside." "They are white on the inside." "They have little black seeds." "They crunch when you bite them," etc.

Pictures of apples and other items can now be presented to the children, while the actual objects remain in view. The children can be asked to identify each picture as "an apple" or "not an apple." If they can say, "It's not an apple, it's a banana," that is fine, but they should not be forced to learn the names of the objects that are not apples at this point.

Obviously, the procedure of the lesson will vary somewhat according to what word the teacher wants the children to learn. A lesson on names of shapes might include a walk around the school or neighborhood to locate additional examples of things that are "round," and "not round"; or children might cut out "round" and "not round" shapes from magazines, or mold "round" and "not round" shapes from clay. A lesson on relational terms might end with a game of "Simon Says"; e.g., "Simon says sit on top of your desk; Simon says sit under your desk; Simon says stand behind your desk; put your hand on top of your desk," etc.

In addition to these kinds of variations, the lesson on apples can be followed up by a series of lessons that help children to differentiate among various other classes or subclasses. Several more oranges could be added to the group of items, and children could be asked to differentiate between "oranges" and "not oranges." In this process, it can be pointed out that apples are one kind of "not oranges."

As another variation, "fruit" can be separated from "not fruit," and "things we eat" from "not things we eat." In this process, children can be introduced to terms connected with the language of classification, such as "group," "subgroup," "characteristic," "criteria." Thus, lessons dealing with names of concrete objects can lead into lessons that develop language essential to the logical processes that children are developing at this period.

129

A somewhat different technique, but a favorite method of introducing new words to children, is the use of a field trip. There is some merit in this method, in that it relates new words to a concrete experience. However, the standard type of field trip leaves much to be desired in terms of language learning.

For one thing, the adult-child ratio is usually too low, with two or three adults supervising twenty-five or thirty children. For another thing, the group of children attending is frequently too large. In many schools it is policy for all the first grades to go together on any given field trip. In this kind of a situation, the focus is on having children look and listen rather than having them comment or ask questions. Adult effort is directed toward keeping the children in line, stopping fights, and counting heads. There is no time to pay attention to or discuss individual interests that might be sparked by what the children are seeing. In a large group, many children cannot get a clear view of whatever is being observed, many cannot hear what the teacher or guide is saying, and many are distracted by other children. None of this is conducive to language learning.

To get more benefit from field trips, we recommend that the adult-child ratio be kept as low as one to three or one to four. These small groups should circulate about the store (or farm or museum or zoo) independently, pausing to discuss whatever impresses them most. Children should be encouraged to talk about what they see, and adults should supply names or terms for things that are new to them.

During the course of the trip, pictures should be taken. These could be super-8 mm films or slides or Polaroid snapshots, depending on what is being observed, what equipment is available, and the skills of the teacher. Once the children are back in the classroom, these pictures will serve to help them recall their experience. They will provide a focal point for additional discussion and for the introduction or reinforcement of new terms.

This kind of field trip encourages informal individual conversation. The pictures provide an opportunity for a more formal or structured setting in which common language learnings related to the field trip can be emphasized.

Another way of handling a field trip is to have each small group observe one thing that is unique—that is, that is *not* observed by any of the other groups. This can be arranged through careful pre-planning by the teacher and is easily done in connection with visits to large museums.

Upon their return, each group would then be responsible for reporting upon what they saw and learned in their unique sidetrip. These reports would be illustrated with the pictures taken during the trip, and on a subsequent trip to the same museum, which would occur within a week of the first trip, children would have an opportunity to see the exhibits that interested them most from the reports they had heard.

In this way, children are given a reason to communicate with each other and a purpose for listening to each other. At the same time, they are developing the attitude that many subjects are worthy of a second look. Finally, the new terms that have been developed in connection with the first field trip are reinforced and practiced during discussions of the second trip.

It might be well to point out that new vocabulary is developed in all subject areas, not just in the language arts program. Each field of study has its own language that includes terms related to materials or equipment that are used, to techniques, procedures, or operations that are learned, and to concepts that are developed. This kind of language learning will occur in formal situations, such as the reading and mathematics lessons, and in informal situations, such as the uncommon learning centers. It is an important part of the concerted effort to increase children's vocabulary.

INCREASING ORAL COMMUNICATION

A second area of concern in planning language activities for inner-city children is finding means of increasing the children's active use of oral communication. Much of the available research stresses the "nonverbal" nature of the disadvantaged child. Student teachers, supervised by the authors, have frequently fretted, when working with black children, about the fact that the children answer questions with nods or monosyllables, and that they "do not use complete sentences."

We find these reports hard to reconcile with the recorded conversations of black children, such as those published in *The School Children*.[1] We suspect that many children in the inner city have learned to be highly verbal in their relationships with peers and to be nonverbal in their relationships with adults. Teachers, as well as parents, have contributed to this learning, for in the average classroom, the rewards go to the quiet child who waits his turn or speaks when he is spoken to.

The teacher who wants to increase children's oral communication must encourage conversation in the classroom. This means encouraging a higher noise level in the classroom. It also means the teacher himself must become less verbal in order to provide more time for the children to talk. In short, the teacher who wants to change children's verbal behavior must first change his own verbal behavior.

Talking or not talking is basically a social behavior rather than an intellectual behavior. There is ample evidence to indicate that those who have little to say in general conversation are often the ones who are doing a lot of thinking. They are quiet, not because they do not know what to say, but because they have learned to play the role of listener. The converse also holds true. Those who talk a great deal may or may not be doing a lot of clear thinking, but they have learned to play the role of active talker.

Since the amount of talking one does in a social situation is a kind of social behavior and is a learned behavior, it is also a behavior that can be changed. In an earlier chapter, the process of such change, called behavior modification, was discussed in some detail. It is only necessary here to indicate how the procedure can be applied to the particular behavior desired.

[1] M. F. Greene and O. Ryan, *The School Children*, New York, Pantheon Books, 1966.

If the goal is to increase children's active use of oral communication, then the teacher will want to reward or reinforce the following kinds of appropriate behavior: questions or comments to neighbors during individual work sessions; answers to teacher questions; questions asked of the teacher; comments or suggestions initiated by the student without prior teacher questions; conversations with adult visitors to the classroom; conversations with adults and other students in the lunch room or while walking in the halls. In this endeavor, the teacher will need the cooperation of other school personnel, such as the secretary, the custodian, the cafeteria workers, the paraprofessionals, the teachers' aides, and the PTA volunteers. Most of all, perhaps, he will need the support and approval of his fellow teachers and of the principal. In relation to this particular problem, a quiet school does not lead to better learning.

In addition to rewarding children for talking, the teacher will need to arrange for situations that are conducive to conversation. The teacher who says, "We don't have time for a free period; there is too much these children need to learn," is really shortchanging the children in the long run. A program that provides children with many informal settings and that gives them concrete experiences and individualized experiences places children in an environment that encourages them to talk and gives them something to talk about. Thus, activities mentioned previously, such as field trips with unique side-trips, uncommon learning centers, and scholarship days, are all aspects of the program that can contribute to the increase of active oral communication.

One other technique that the teacher needs to cultivate is the use of the pause in formal lessons. Studies of teacher talk seem to indicate that pauses in the verbal interaction between student and teacher are relatively infrequent. Arno Bellack, for example, found that the average rate of classroom conversation in formal lessons was 1.9 teaching cycles per minute.[2] (A teaching cycle was defined as a unit of pedagogical moves beginning with a structuring or solicitation and ending before new structuring or new solicitation is initiated.) This means, for example, that the average teacher devotes all of thirty seconds to asking a question, getting a response, and commenting on the response. The pace of classroom conversation, apparently, is quite rapid. This pressure for quick comments is contrary to most of what is known about creative thinking and precise speaking.

M. A. Wallach and N. Kogan, in their studies of children's thinking, found that the quick response tended to be the common, cliché-type response.[3] Original, creative responses were slow to be produced, and they increased in number when creative children were given plenty of time to respond. When children in the classroom are pressured to give rapid-fire answers to questions, those answers tend to be both brief and unimaginative.

[2] Arno Bellack et al., *The Language of the Classroom*, Part Two, New York, Teachers College, Columbia University, 1965, p. 151.
[3] *Modes of Thinking in Young Children*, New York, Holt, Rinehart and Winston, 1965, pp. 64–66.

Consider, in addition, the fact that young children in the inner city are still in the early processes of developing a "school" vocabulary. Observe a 4- or 5-year-old from a middle-class background, and you will note that his conversation is frequently halting while he tries to remember a word or phrase he has recently learned. The adult listener must be rather patient to persevere in an extended conversation with such a child. The tendency is for the adult to feed words to the child or to direct the child's comments by questioning.

Similarly, the teacher's tendency is to try to speed up or direct the flow of words in the classroom. If a child does not answer a question rather quickly, most teachers will repeat or reword the question or, perhaps, suggest that some other child help out with the answer. Thus, the child who attempts to think through an answer or to recall a specific word in order to make the answer more precise is often penalized.

The teacher who wants to encourage children to talk more must learn to ask a question and then *wait*. A teacher is not a radio announcer. In the classroom, the sound of silence can indicate that thoughtful comments are being stimulated and constructed. This is a highly desirable atmosphere for the encouragement of active oral communication.

INCREASING AWARENESS OF ENGLISH STRUCTURE

The third area of concern in a language program for inner-city children is the planning of activities that will increase children's awareness of the structure of the English language and that will encourage them to make use of a greater variety of structural patterns. In the first grade, this formal study of language structure will be of an introductory nature. It will not be extensive in scope, but it will be highly important, since it forms the basis for later language learning.

We recommended earlier the use of Gattegno's Words in Color for the first-grade reading program. This program includes several kinds of activities related to language structure. We should like to describe some of them here.

One of the materials used in this program is a set of word cards. These cards contain words the children have learned or will learn. The words are printed in black, but the cards are colored; each color corresponding to a particular grammatical function. Thus, words used as nouns appear on green cards, and words used as verbs appear on orange cards.

Children can be given a set of cards of various colors containing words they know. They can work alone to try to build sentences with these cards, or they can work in pairs and take turns adding words. A sentence thus constructed might read: "Her (white) sister (green) fell (orange) down (red) some (white) stairs (green), but (beige) she (white) was (orange) not (blue) hurt (yellow)." Attempts to continue adding words lead children to use more complex constructions.

Variations on this suggested by Gattegno include having one child think of a sentence and put down several words of the sentence, leaving some blank spaces. The other child then fills in the gaps, and the completed sentence is compared with the one originally imagined. The total class can also play a variation of the sentence-building game. One child puts a word card on the board, and the others try to think of sentences containing this word. Another child adds a word to help form a sentence of which he has thought. The class must then try to think of sentences containing these two words. As additional cards are added, the cards may be rearranged.

A variation that Gattegno does not suggest is to give children a pattern of colors and have them construct several sentences using the same pattern. The pattern "white, green, orange, green" could produce sentences such as: "Their dog learned tricks"; "Both boys eat potatoes"; "Some teachers are men." Varying the pattern will give children practice in building varieties of sentences. For this kind of exercise, however, the teacher needs to select the cards to be used with some care, so that children are able to build several sentences but do not have to work with unwieldy numbers of cards.

Another type of activity suggested by Gattegno is to have children remove words from a sentence one by one and still have the sentence say something. Attention can be directed to the colors of the words that remain, and gradually children begin to note that some patterns, such as "green, orange," are repeated rather frequently.

This realization can be followed up by attempts to vary sentences, keeping one or two words constant. Thus, children might be asked to find orange words that can pattern after "Her cat," or they could look for green words that might pattern before "is funny."

Another useful activity with the word cards can give children practice with sentence transformations. Given a sentence such as "The sky is cloudy," children can be asked to change it into a question. A series of sentences of this type will help to make children aware that the orange word changes position in this transformation.

Similarly, they can be asked to change a sentence such as "It is raining," to mean that it happened yesterday or that it will happen tomorrow. As they work through several sentences, children will begin to notice that the orange word changes form. As awareness grows, children can be introduced to the appropriate words, such as "verb," "tense," "past," "present," "future." These words will have meaning if work with the word cards along the lines suggested has preceded their use.

The basic procedures with the word cards include building up sentences word by word, decomposing sentences word by word, transforming sentences (from statement to question, from affirmative to negative, from past to present, from singular to plural, etc.), building sentences that follow particular color patterns, and changing sentence meaning by substituting different words of the same color. These procedures can be followed with individual students, small groups, or the total class. Thus, a variety of activities are available to the teacher.

134

The major advantage of the word cards is that they help to make the initial study of language structure more concrete. Children can manipulate the cards and see the difference in results, as well as hearing the difference. The use of color helps to make children aware of standard sentence patterns and transformations. This awareness should give them more control over their own use of language. Most important of all, perhaps, the practice in manipulating sentences and cards helps children to feel that language is something that they can control or with which they can play. Thus, feelings of success develop out of these experiences, and freedom comes a little closer.

WORKING WITH BILINGUAL CHILDREN

A special language problem exists when students are bilingual or speak a language other than English, and this is a very real problem in many inner-city schools, with Spanish being the language usually involved. There is evidence to indicate that young children learn a second language much more readily than do adults, and the approved pattern of teaching foreign languages today is to "immerse" the student in the oral language; e.g., Spanish classes are conducted entirely in Spanish. These two facts have combined to establish a pattern of dealing with bilingual children in the elementary schools by putting them into classes in which only English is spoken and expecting them to learn English, reading, spelling, mathematics, science, and social studies, all of which are taught to them in a language they do not understand.

This is immersion carried to the extreme, and it has a harmful side effect. As children learn the English language, they also learn that they are stupid, because they have trouble learning reading, spelling, mathematics, etc. Such a program tends to destroy the child's desire to succeed by teaching him very early that he is unable to succeed.

An alternative that has been tried with some success is to run a special bilingual classroom for bilingual children. In this classroom, all subjects are taught in two languages. A statement in English is followed by the same statement in Spanish. Thus, a child is able to separate his understanding of the subject from his understanding of the second language. Subject-matter learning and desire to succeed are both facilitated.

To some people, this kind of separation smacks of segregated classes. It has another disadvantage as well. Since all children in the class have learned Spanish as a first language, the informal conversation tends to be Spanish, and opportunities for practicing English are lost.

We suggest mixing Spanish- and English-speaking children in one classroom and conducting special formal lessons for the bilingual children in a bilingual manner. This can be done fairly easily with the grouping system used in the reading and mathematics curricula. In the language arts program, instruction will vary from individual to group to total-class work. When grouping is used, a bilingual group can be formed. When the total class works

135

together, the teacher can make additional comments, as they seem necessary, to bilingual children.

In the informal settings, such as snack, play, lunch, and work in the uncommon learning centers, every effort should be made to encourage conversation between Spanish- and English-speaking children. These informal situations can do a great deal to enrich the language environment of the bilingual children, as well as the monolingual children.

This type of dual organization utilizes the strengths of both the aforementioned approaches to the problem of bilingual children. In an informal setting where there is less academic pressure, children are immersed in the second language. In formal instructional settings where understanding is crucial and performance counts, children are taught in a bilingual manner.

SUMMARY

The language arts program for first grade, which has been briefly described in this chapter, grows out of a view of language as a basic tool in the process of thinking as well as the process of communication. If this view is accepted, it follows that language instruction must provide opportunity for using language in appropriate kinds of communication (e.g., conversation, argument, oral reports) and appropriate kinds of thinking (e.g., classifying objects, observing and describing, weighing alternative choices of words or phrases). The activities suggested are an attempt to provide these kinds of opportunities, always keeping in mind that the child needs to succeed if desire for learning is to be enhanced.

ELEVEN: KNOWING HOW TO DEVELOP LINGUISTIC GENERALIZATIONS

The emphasis of the kindergarten and first-grade language program has been on the development of vocabulary, getting children to express themselves, helping children to use language as a means of communicating, and giving them some experiences with manipulating the structures of the language.

The emphasis on these matters continues in the second grade, and many of the same types of activities can be continued here. In addition, we believe children can profit a great deal from studying language as the linguist does—that is, by exploring and describing the language as it exists. In doing this, we are not merely interested in language study as a pure science. Knowledge about the language is not our only objective. We hope that through bringing knowledge of the language to conscious awareness the children will learn to manipulate the language more effectively.

The authors have conducted a little research that suggests that this is the case with junior high school students,[1] and we have published a text for junior high school youth.[2] The doctoral project of one of the author's was a curriculum proposal for fourth, fifth, and sixth graders in the area of linguistics.[3] Hard data do not presently exist in sufficient amounts to lead one to move forward fully confident that the formal study of linguistics will prove beneficial. One can, however, make the case from another standpoint. It is clear that children have been studying language for some time and have been constructing generalizations about the language and have been applying these generalizations as they use the language. Our proposal is to sharpen or improve the studying skills by teaching the child some appropriate strategies and by organizing the data in suitable amounts so that the rate of learning is increased.

ENCOURAGING GENERALIZATIONS ABOUT LANGUAGE

The procedure we shall use is quite simple. First, we give the children some data, we ask them to draw upon their knowledge of the language in order to add similar data, and then we ask them to construct some generalizations about the data amassed. We then repeat the procedure with some new data and compare to see if any modifications are needed in the earlier generalizations.

We might start our first lesson by asking the children to produce more paired sentences such as the following.

The bird sings.
The birds sing.

The plane flies.
The planes fly.

We would expect the children to offer statements similar to the following.

[1] H. Morine, "The Use of Structural Linguistics to Improve Writing and Language Analysis on the Junior High School Level," final report to the New York State Department of Education, Albany, July, 1962.
[2] N. Postman, H. Morine, and G. Morine, *Discovering Your Language*, New York, Holt, Rinehart and Winston, 1963.
[3] H. Morine, "A Proposal for the Teaching of Linguistics in Grades Four, Five, and Six, unpublished doctoral dissertation, Teachers College, Columbia University, New York, 1962.

The dog barks.	**The man runs.**
The dogs bark.	**The men run.**
The cat eats.	**The house burns.**
The cats eat.	**The houses burn.**

As we write each of these on the board, we would read them aloud. Language is oral and it is the speech we wish to study, not the orthography. Following are the generalizations the children might produce from the data collected:

1. When the second word means one of something, the third word ends with an "s" sound.
2. When the second word means more than one, the third word doesn't end in an "s" sound.

These two generalizations may not be seen immediately. Suppose the data included only the following or only pairs in the following form.

The girl runs.	**The car runs.**
The girls run.	**The cars run.**
The cat eats.	**The teachers talk.**
The cats eat.	**The teacher talks.**
The boy laughs.	**The bird sings.**
The boys laugh.	**The birds sing.**

Given these data, the generalizations could be accurately stated as follows:

1. When the second word has an "s" sound on the end, the third word doesn't have an "s" sound.
2. When the second word doesn't have an "s" sound on the end, the third word will have an "s" sound.

Given this, the teacher would continue to ask for new data and even suggest some himself. When "The man works" and "The men work" is offered, a problem arises—a contradiction is seen. These two sentences seem to be like the others, but they do not fit the generalizations that have been constructed to describe the data. The class must then follow the time-honored strategies of science. In this case, a slight restatement of the generalizations saves the day. By making plurality the key, rather than the "s" sound, an adequate description that holds in all cases is possible. The teacher may come back the next day, however, and offer some data that will create a methodological problem and lead to new discoveries about the language. The teacher says, "On the first three boards are the data we have analyzed in written form to date. On the last board are the two generalizations we produced. Now let me offer you some data that may cause you a problem." The teacher then goes to the board, erases the third word in one pair of sentences, writes the word "slowly" in its place and follows "slowly" with the word that was erased. He continues to do this, sometimes replacing one of the third words in a pair of sentences, sometimes replacing both of them until the board looks as follows. In actual classroom situations there will be many more sentences than are offered here.

The bird slowly sings.	**The dog loudly barks.**
The birds slowly sing.	**The dogs bark.**
The cat eats.	**The man works.**
The cats slowly eat.	**Slowly, the men work.**

The children should see fairly quickly that the terms "second" and "third" are poor designations. It is position that is important. They need some other way of stating the generalizations. Second and third words aren't the crucial variable—or even fourth or fifth words. Some may see that you can change the sentences a great deal and "bird" and "sing" will still change the same way. They may introduce the data, "The big red bird very slowly sings a sad song," and observe that if they change "bird" to "birds" then "sings" changes to "sing."

This kind of data and strategy should bring them to see that it isn't "bird" and "sings" or "cat" and "eats" that are related. Rather, one kind of event, of which "bird" and "cat" are examples, is related to another kind of event, of which "sings" and "eats" are examples. They may then look for characteristics that tell them what kind of event something is. "Bird" and "cat," for example, can replace each other, and there can be one or more of them. They cannot take the place of "sings" or "eats," and should they be used in a way similar to "The eats disappeared," the meaning of "eats" has changed. This discussion should lead to a fuller discovery of the parts of speech: how nouns are connected to verbs, and how verbs can reveal the number of the noun.

The generalizations will have to be modified to read, "When the noun is singular, an 's' sound ends the verb," and, "When the noun is plural, the 's' sound doesn't end the verb."

The teacher can force a generalization relating verbs to time and further force the inclusion of time in the two generalizations we have been giving attention by offering the following pair of sentences: "The boy ate"; "The boys ate." Again, the strategy is to offer data that force a contradiction between the generalizations constructed and the data. In accommodating the two, the children learn something new about the language and about the learning process.

The strategy of the teacher and the strategy he is demonstrating for the children is the one of constructing a generalization that describes the data and then looking for data that would contradict the generalization, thereby forcing a rejection or modification of the generalization. Description has to do with the constructing of categories or classes and the construction of state-

140

ments (generalizations) that show how the categories are functionally related to each other. We thus have statements at two levels or of two kinds: statements that spell out the criteria to be used to test the category to which a word belongs, and statements that describe the functional relationships of the categories, classes, or if you prefer, parts of speech.

The teacher should not expect a rapid statement of generalizations from children. Indeed, some second graders will not be intellectually ready to state generalizations on their own. Those who are able to do this will still profit from a good deal of preliminary "playing" with the data.

As we mentioned in our discussion of the mathematics program, there is evidence to suggest that forcing an early verbalization of an idea can tend to inhibit further development of that idea. Thus, the generalizations outlined above would not grow out of one or two lessons. Development of such a series of generalizations might better be viewed as a unit of work to be dealt with over a period of weeks.

Before verbalization of a generalization occurs, children should be able to demonstrate that they can apply the rule. This ability develops as they handle the data intensively. Thus, children might fill up several blackboards and several pages of their notebooks with pairs of sentences such as: "The cat purrs. The cats purr." The teacher can add some sentences to spark further ideas, such as: "The locomotive puffs. The locomotives puff." "The worm wiggles. The worms wiggle."

After collecting tons of examples, children who are aware of the rule can demonstrate this awareness by filling in the blanks in sentences such as the following:

The ball bounces.	**The balls**_____.
The ship sinks.	**The ships** _____.
The bird _____.	**The birds dive.**

When they can demonstrate ability to apply the generalization, then the next step is to be able to verbalize it or to understand it when someone else verbalizes it.

The extra time required and the additional data used in this process yield some other important benefits, beyond the final statement of a generalization, that are consistent with our end. Children become aware of various spelling patterns in connection with noun plurality when they collect large numbers of sentences such as the following:

The lady eats.	**The ox pulls.**
The ladies eat.	**The oxen pull.**
The cockroach runs.	**The deer leaps.**
The cockroaches run.	**The deer leap.**

Indeed rather than leave this learning to chance, the teacher does well to suggest that the children reorganize the data into groups of sentences that reveal these differences and from which we might be able to develop some spelling generalizations.

Another benefit may well be that children begin to listen to language around them more carefully in an attempt to get new ideas for sentences. In the process, they will quite probably add some new words to their vocabularies. These benefits will not be achieved if the teacher pushes children toward an early verbalization of the generalization.

SUGGESTED LANGUAGE EXPERIENCES

Keeping in mind, then, that the best procedure is to have children collect a great deal of data and to give them time to let these data "sink in," let us outline some additional kinds of language experiences in which second graders will be involved. We could offer children the following data:

Those boy eats.	An elephant runs.
Those boys eat.	An elephant run.
Some boy ran home.	The boy runs.
Some boys ran home.	The boys run.
A boy ran home.	Every boy eat.
A boys ran home.	Every boy eats.
All boy ran home.	One cat eats.
All boys ran home.	One cats eat.
Few girls eat.	Two boy eats.
Few girl eats.	Two boys eat.
Many boy eats.	Three boys eat.
Many boys eat.	Three boy eats.

The first thing the children will observe and test is that some of the sentences are not English and yet they are English. That is, we don't say, "A boys ran home." If we say "a," we must say "boy." Some of the data will be rejected. With the data that are left, the children will come to recognize that "all," "these," "those," "the," "some," "an," "few," "a," "many," "every," "one," and "two" are in the same category. They will realize further that the category is functionally related to nouns in that these words can be a clue as to number. Some of these words signify singularity and some signify plurality, while others may pattern with a noun whether the noun is singular or plural. They may see further that this class of events is always followed by a noun before an utterance is completed. They can be led to see later in the study of the language that, while an adjective may pattern between this group of words and a noun, a verb will not.

There are about thirty-three words that are in this particular class or category (called determiners), and children should be asked to see how many they can discover. This can be done by having a model sentence or two in view, with the determiner position left blank. Determiners are words that meet the test of patterning in the blank in the sentence, "_____ girl (s) eat," but do not pattern in the blank in the sentence, "The girl(s) is/are _____." The children can list words they find that meet these criteria. The above can be handled in several steps, with children first listing words that fit in "_____ girl eats" and "_____ girls eat." They can then take this list and see which words do not fit in "The girls are _____" or "The girl is _____."

Adjectives are words that pattern in the blanks in the sentences, "The girl(s) is/are _____" and "The _____ girl runs." When working with adjectives, much time should be devoted to listing them. We once taught this lesson in the spring of the year to a first-grade class in an inner-city school as part of a one-week unit on language. We introduced this lesson on the second day and got from the children a list of seven words. Included in the list was the word "delectable," which a youngster heard on television and, as she put it, "Sounds so nice." The third lesson was devoted to exploring various noun positions, and the fourth lesson was devoted to exploring adverbial positions. On the fifth day, we returned to our two adjective positions and the children listed ninety-three of them in a forty-minute period.

There are a number of possible explanations as to what happened to produce this dramatic change in performance. The one we believe best fits the facts includes these propositions. Simply because language had been selected as something to study, a phenomenon of which no one had previously thought was focused upon; i.e., the children were sensitized to the problem of language and language learning. By studying nouns, verbs, adjectives, adverbs, and by then returning to each of them in order, criteria of two kinds were being developed. Criteria of the first type state that a particular class of words patterns in such-and-such a position, or that a particular class of words has such-and-such a characteristic. These types of statements come from studying the class of words in question. The second kind of criteria state that a particular class of words doesn't pattern in such-and-such a position and doesn't have such-and-such a characteristic. The second kind of criteria, or test, can come only from comparing statements of the first kind made about two different classes of words. Thus, the children may observe that adjectives as well as determiners pattern in the blank in the sentence, "_____ boy(s) run(s) fast," but only adjectives pattern in the blank in the sentence, "The _____ boy(s) run(s) fast," or in the sentence, "The boy(s) is/are _____." To put it all another way, one's understanding of how adjectives pattern and function is in large part contingent upon understanding how nouns, verbs, and adverbs pattern and function. It is analogous to understanding the number five through understanding one, two, three, four, six, seven, two plus three, eight minus three, two times two plus one, the concepts of prime and composite numbers. The meaning of each part of speech cannot be understood through studying that part of speech alone. As more and more of the total structure of language is studied, more and more light is cast upon the individual parts. The converse is also true. Therefore, the teaching strategy or the learning strategy is to move from part to part, from part to whole, and from whole to part. Just as "five" cannot be completely understood through analyzing five in complete isolation, a part of speech cannot be studied in isolation.

Adverbs may be studied by asking children to offer words that pattern in the blank in the sentence, "The man walked _____." The children can then work to make a list for the sentence, "The man _____ walked," and follow with, "_____, the man walked." They will discover some differences in how these words pattern. A word like "slowly" will pattern in all three positions. A word like "in" or "down" will not.

At this point, the four *form classes* (to use Charles Fries' terminology for the categories of words that correspond roughly to nouns, verbs, adjectives, and adverbs), as well as determiners, will have been explored.[4] These should be reexplored toward the following ends: One, to find new positions that the five parts of speech studied can hold. Two, to discover new characteristics about each part of speech. Three, to develop some propositions, though not necessarily verbalized propositions, that reveal the relationships of the five parts of speech to each other.

SAMPLE EXERCISES

Below are some illustrative exercises that can be used to organize data so that children can make some valid observations about the English language.

EXERCISE ONE.
What kinds of words go in the blanks in the following sentences:
1. The _____ girl has a _____ hairdo.
2. _____, the _____ boy went to school.
3. The man fixed _____ door of _____ car.
4. Many tall _____ are brown.
5. The boy _____ all day.

EXERCISE TWO.
Using the words below, construct an English sentence.
1. elephant, large, has, ears, the
2. small, a, yellow, picturesque, house, a, on, hill, is
3. rain, falls, the, lightly

EXERCISE THREE.
What part of speech is "flump" in each of the sentences below:
1. The girl is flumpy.
2. Flumpily, the house flumped.
3. The flump is for sale.
4. The boy flumped his flump bicycle.

[4] C. C. Fries, *The Structure of English*, New York, Harcourt, Brace and Co., 1952.

144

EXERCISE FOUR.

Think of three words that will pattern in each of the blanks in the following paragraph.

       _____ a _____ girl _____ dressed for _____. _____ knew she mustn't be late, but her _____ dress was dirty and she didn't want to wear the dress with the _____ on it. She knew that _____ girls were _____ on time and _____ to do the best they could in _____.

EXERCISE FIVE.

List as many words as you can that have the same ending as the underlined word and that pattern in the position of the underlined word.

1. The <u>commotion</u> was great.
2. We own a <u>beautiful</u> dog.
3. The <u>hiker</u> was tired.
4. The <u>happiest</u> girl I know is Maria.
5. <u>Slowly,</u> the artist painted a portrait.
6. The teacher <u>talked</u> slowly.

By the time these lessons have started, children should have agreed upon names for the various parts of speech they have studied. For our purposes here, we shall use the symbols N (noun), V (verb), A (adjective), ADV (adverb), and D (determiner).[5]

EXERCISE SIX.

Construct an English sentence for each of the following patterns.

1. D N V.
2. D A N V.
3. D A A N V.
4. D A A A N V.
5. D A A A A N V.
6. V D N.
7. V D A N.
8. V D A A N.
9. A N V ADV.
10. ADV D A N V.
11. ADV D A N Ved into D N.
12. ADV D A A N Ved into D A N.
13. ADV D A A N Ved into D A A N with D A N.
14. In D N by D N D A N Ved ADV over to D A N.

The lessons above are meant to be illustrative. Many more problems need to be included for each type of exercise. As the children gain facility in handling each type of exercise, the difficulty of the exercise can be increased. The difficulty of Exercise One is increased by offering fewer and fewer concrete clues, until sentences similar to the following are posed:

---

[5] Teachers who feel that the new vocabulary load is already quite high for their children may wish to continue using the color names for the parts of speech that the children learned in first grade in connection with the Words in Color reading program.

97. In _____ _____, _____ girls, _____ly _____ to finish their _____
_____.

98. The _____ _____ _____ _____ into the _____ _____ _____.

The difficulty of Exercise Two can be increased by increasing the number of words and by using words unfamiliar to the children. The way these lessons are increased in difficulty forces the child to draw on and develop his knowledge of how the syntactical structure of the language helps to convey the meaning of the language.

The same end can be accomplished through extending the number of "flumps" used in Exercise Three:

27. The flump flumped flumpingly.

Exercise Six can be given another dimension by having the children construct a number of sentences for a particular pattern, by lengthening the pattern, and by having the children construct patterns for their classmates to try. The latter will force the question, "Is such-and-such a pattern?" The proof is that someone can construct an English sentence for the pattern. These exercises force children to the position that word order is important in English. They also give children much useful practice in constructing lengthy sentences that lead to more precision in writing, some development of writing style, and more understanding of the nuances of language structure.

PREPOSITIONS AND CONJUNCTIONS

Some of the lessons have anticipated the treatment of prepositions. This class of words can be developed by asking children to list all of the words that pattern in the blank spaces in the following sentences.

The man fell _____ the bed.
The girls ran _____ the house.

It is worth noting that, in constructing any of these lists, some words will be put on the list quite readily. It is predictable that "in," "into," and "on" will appear near the beginning of the list and that they will be familiar to all of the children. "Through," "underneath," and a few others will not be forthcoming so readily. The teacher should, however, know all of the words in the determiner, conjunction, and preposition classes. Given this, he is in a position to do two things that will enable the children to learn to handle these less-familiar words with facility. One, he can use them in his speech, and two, he can use them in the exercises above, making sure that he doesn't include them in the first dozen examples of each exercise, as this may lead to the child failing to complete the exercise for the wrong reasons.

The teaching of conjunctions can be handled in a manner similar to prepositions and determiners, but it is, perhaps, useful to do some additional things to reveal the relational or logical function of conjunctions. Conjunctions may be introduced by asking children to complete the following sentences, using a new word in the first blank each time.

It rained yesterday _____ we _____.
The following sentences might result:

It rained yesterday, and we were sad.
It rained yesterday, or we would have gone on a picnic.
It rained yesterday, but we didn't get wet.
It rained yesterday after we got home from school.
It rained yesterday, so we waded in the puddles.

There are a number of other words that can pattern in the blank above or in similar sentences. "Therefore," "however," "although," "moreover," "then," "thus," "because," and "since" may not be suggested by the children, though the suggestion of the last two would not surprise us. "Therefore," "however," "although" and "then," as well as "because" and "since," are very useful words that help to make communication more precise in that they enable the child to express with economy a relationship he has in mind. We, therefore, would like to see the child who can handle the logical relationship be equipped with the language necessary to express the relationship. Some of these relationships develop earlier than others, and not all second graders have developed all of the logical abilities that these words illustrate. Briefly, the situation relating to these rather complex phenomena of language, thought, and the relationship between the two is as follows:

One, the child can understand a logical relationship and have the language to express it. Most second graders will, for example, have a notion of combining and can use the term "and" to express it. They will also have the notion of "or," as well as the term in their vocabulary when "or" refers to one or the other but not both, as it does when it is used disjunctively.

Two, the child may have the term in his vocabulary but may not use it in the logical sense. He may use it in the psychological sense as "because" is used in the sentence, "It rained yesterday because I was a bad boy."

Three, the child has the logical relationship in mind but doesn't have the vocabulary to communicate the relationship directly. Diane Arnell, a student at Hofstra University, discovered and reported in an unpublished paper that 15-year-old deaf children couldn't complete the sentence, "It rained yesterday, therefore _____." Miss Arnell then gave them three endings for the sentence. Three weeks later she gave the same children the sentence, "They studied last week, therefore _____," and each of the children readily supplied a large number of completions for the sentence. The explanation we offer for this is that deaf children have limited experiences with language, and even after they lip read, many people will tend to simplify their language constructions when speaking to them because they assume the child who cannot hear cannot understand. The result is that the children have had no experience with the words "therefore," "however," and "although." It is just these words with which the young disadvantaged child is liable to be unfamiliar.

Given these three possible situations, and given that we wish to teach these

147

words only if they will allow the child to express with economy a logical relationship he has in mind, we suggest the following procedures for teaching these words.

Give a model for the child to copy.

He lost the race, although he ran fast.

Ask the children to complete the following:

She is very thin, although _____ _____ _____ _____ _____.

Have them contribute their endings and put them on the board. Have them examine the proposed sentences to see if they are all acceptable English. Make minor corrections without any fuss, and note those sentences upon which the children disagree. Then offer the class, "Although he is small, _____ _____ _____ _____." List these completions on the board. The teacher should erase the board after briefly discussing the new completions.

The following day, ask each child to try to produce two completions for each of the following:

I am tired today, although _____.
Although most cats clean themselves, _____.

The teacher should collect these papers from the children and, when he has an opportunity, examine them to see which children can and which cannot deal with the logic of "although." For those who can handle "although" correctly, additional work should be given that will develop their facility to use it in all of its contexts. "Although" can be followed by a pronoun, a prepositional phrase, or a determiner, and practice using each of these should be given.

Proceeding in the same manner, "therefore," "however," "thus," "then," "if–then," and "either–or" constructions may be introduced. Children who have difficulty shouldn't be pushed. Children who succeed can, of course, be given sophisticated model sentences to reproduce, such as C D A A N P D N V ADV C D V D N P D N, where C is a conjunction and P is a preposition.

TWELVE: LEADING THE WAY ADMINISTRATIVELY

There are essentially two kinds of administrators. One kind is dominated by a "don't-rock-the-boat" philosophy. He values stability at all costs and is primarily concerned with his own survival and the survival of those who support him. Innovation under this kind of administrator is a function of public relations. He always keeps in mind that good public relations and sound politics, with indifferent innovation, are preferable to sound programs that make a difference in the education of children but are poor public relations and unsound politics.

The other type of administrator gives leadership. Where the "don't-rock-the-boat" administrator is thinking of reasons why something can't be done, this type of leader is saying, "Let's do it. We'll figure out how to overcome some of the objections to the plan when the time comes. Perhaps we can even find a way of turning it to the advantage of sound education." Where the first type of administrator thinks about retiring in his present position or a "better" position, the leader takes it as axiomatic that the chances are high that somewhere along the line he will have to take a stand on principle and will probably go down to defeat. He is a hardheaded realist and an optimist. He gives of himself, demands of others, and believes that what he is doing can make a difference to those who attend his school.

The establishment of a program such as we have proposed calls for the second kind of administrator. The purpose of this chapter is to give suggestions to those who would dare to try to make a difference. Let those who would try remember that the first kind of administrator will probably fight against and try to destroy what is being attempted. It has been that way since the first professional status-quo administrator was trained.

Before the program we have proposed can be fully operative, the following tasks must be faced and completed. We believe they must be handled in the approximate sequence that follows.[1]

1. The development of a clear understanding of what is theoretically involved in the program.
2. The hiring of two supervisors who also understand and are willing to support the program.
3. The selection of eight kindergarten teachers, four first-grade teachers, and six second-grade teachers. In some cases these may be personnel already employed in the school.
4. A thoroughgoing discussion and study of the proposed curriculum and its means of implementation.
5. A presentation to the PTA and other interested groups.
6. The hiring of paraprofessionals.
7. The summer training of paraprofessionals in perception, reading, and mathematics.
8. The hiring of teachers' aides in August.
9. The administration of the early stages of curriculum implementation in September, October, November, and December of the first year.
10. The presentation of a progress report to the PTA.
11. The setting up of the uncommon learning centers.

[1] The reader must understand that different situations will call for different responses. We cannot, of course, anticipate and respond to all of these. We can only draw on our own experiences and the experiences of others who have made innovations. As we move through this chapter, we shall suggest propositions that we have found are the ones most likely to yield success if followed. We recognize, further, that each leader has his own style and his own psychological dimensions that tend to limit what he can or cannot do.

12. The supervision of centers.
13. The presentation of the first scholarship week.
14. An evaluation of the program as developed to date.
15. The development of plans for the second year.

PRELIMINARY TASKS

Several statements seem relevant to us regarding the first step. We believe that the reason the professionally trained administrator is frequently so ineffective is that he has been trained in means. The effective leader must be trained in ends. He must, therefore, fully understand the program he is about to initiate. In the case of this particular proposal, he must read Gattegno's *Teaching Reading with Words In Color*, study the charts and worksheets, and read *Background and Principles*. He must then find a nonreader and teach him to read, using the Words in Color method. The would-be administrator of this proposal must read the literature on behavior modification and try it out in the classroom. He must read in order to understand something of how to teach with the Cuisenaire rods; he must play with them by the hour, discuss them with others, and teach with them. He should probably read Fries' *The Structure of English* and the teacher's edition of *Discovering Your Language*, by Postman, Morine, and Morine. He would do well to read Kephart's *The Slow Learner in the Classroom* in order to gain a feel for the theoretical basis of the perception program we have proposed. He must then reflect long and hard on the pedagogy we have proposed in this book. He must come to know it intellectually, and at the gut level he must come to believe it will work.

He must do the above for several reasons. One, only through this kind of thoroughness can he know how to hire and train staff. Two, just as children know when teachers are in doubt, staff and parents often know when the administrator is in doubt. It is only through thorough knowledge that the leader can have the conviction necessary to carry the rest through a new and, to them, undemonstrated program. Three, the explanation for successes and failures of the program lies within the theoretical formulations of the program. Four, the solution to the practical problems of day-to-day operation lies within the theoretical foundations of the program. Five, it is essential to thoroughly know where one wants to go if one is to make decisions that will stand as good ones. Mistakes will inevitably be made. These will usually be the result of judgments made on inadequate knowledge. It is foolish to make mistakes because one doesn't fully know the program he is implementing.

In the process of learning the program, the leader should spend some time discussing what he is reading and teaching with individuals who might make supervisors in the program. The characteristics one needs in supervisors are intellectual breadth and depth, an ability to teach adults, a sense of humor, toughmindedness, a willingness to work overtime to make a mediocre teacher a great one, enough detachment to be able to admit afterward

151

that he has failed, a desire to understand and be a part of the total operation, and a drive to someday be an innovative leader himself. Good supervisors must be thinkers, they must be ethical, and they must be willing to sink or swim with the program. No single act is more important than the hiring of the supervisors. A poor paraprofessional can temporarily hurt 24 children a half hour each day. A poor supervisor can hurt 288 children all day long.

Supervisors must be paid well, and the innovative leader may have to search far and wide to get them. He will draw on the local community for his teachers' aides and paraprofessionals. But in hiring teachers and supervisors, whether or not they come from the inner-city is not the issue; nor is their color, religion, or economic status. The crucial variable is their scholarship, their perceptiveness, their ability to handle people, and their ability to teach. The law of supply and demand may force the hiring of a supervisor who still has some things to learn. It must never be forgotten, however, that the assumption is that teacher aides, paraprofessionals, and to a lesser extent, teachers will be trained to do a particular job. Supervisors, on the other hand, are presumed to be trained already and capable of their job assignment. If they don't know something they need to know, they will have to learn it by staying up nights, not by learning on the job.

The working relationship between leader and supervisors must include the following kinds of rules or guidelines. One, time must be made for quiet after-hour discussions on strategies. Two, decisions should be arrived at jointly whenever possible. When this is not possible, the leader makes the decision. All must recognize that the leader must face the consequences of decisions. Three, the leader must handle political problems. They are not the supervisor's worry. Good supervisors want to work at the job, not handle the chairman of the PTA program committee. Four, once a decision is made that a supervisor will handle problem X, the leader must give that supervisor the freedom to exercise his own judgments, and he must facilitate solutions at the direction of the supervisor.

The concept of leadership we have says, in part, that the leader hires the best people he can to do a particular task. He then goes to work for the people he has hired to ensure that they get every opportunity to accomplish the task in the manner they judge to be the best. Many administrators don't understand this, or worse, they fear it. The result is that no one is free to do anything.

The hiring of teachers is a difficult task. Letters of recommendation, unless one knows the writer rather well, are next to useless. A leader enters, in effect, into a contract with his teachers. To do this, each must know what he can expect from the other. Despite our many criticisms of teachers, we are fond of many of them. Schools of education, the community, and others have, in our judgment, misjudged the intent of teachers. Teachers, it seems to us, are, for the most part, not scholars and generally make no claim to be scholars. Many people do claim to be scholars, but few of these people are teachers.

Teachers have, we believe, only a passing interest in understanding methods. They argue about methods and objectives and other matters because we require it of them. Teachers, we believe, are interested in seeing children learn. The satisfaction for a teacher, in most cases, is in the knowledge that he taught a child to read, to compute, to think, to care. A child passed his way and was changed for the better. This is why most teachers teach. They don't teach to prove that learning theory A is a valid theory. They teach because there is satisfaction in helping a child along the way to maturity. They teach for other reasons as well, but for our purpose, this is the crucial one.

If, however, there is satisfaction in saying to one's self, "That child has been helped by me to grow," there is dissatisfaction in saying, "I had her in class for a whole year and didn't do a thing for her. What is to become of her?" There is more than dissatisfaction. There is frustration and demoralization. It is a terrible thing to have a conscience and to fail when the failure hurts a child.

Given this, the contract between the leader and the teacher should be as follows: If you, as teacher, will support the program we are about to describe, we shall daily put our jobs on the line to see that you are successful with each and every child. If you will work with us in a common cause, we shall assist you to become the kind of teacher you thought you would be when you entered the profession. We offer you hard work and a dream. Give us two years, your honest criticism, your professional judgments, your best efforts, and we, in turn, shall give you the same. Among us, we'll educate all who come through the door.

The implications of the above suggest that the hiring process needs to be a little different than the usual. The supervisors and the leader need to screen teachers for flexibility and intelligence (stupid people make lousy teachers). Teachers are entitled to know what is to be taught and how. They should be given materials to read. These materials should then be discussed. The teachers' attitudes toward children and paraprofessionals should be explored. Their stamina and enthusiasm should be assessed. They really shouldn't be told, "Okay, you're hired." In the various exchanges of ideas, a point should be reached where each party recognizes that he wants to work with the other and be a part of "the dream." The teacher comes to a point where he says to himself, "This is what I want to do, and here is where I want to do it." The contract is never spoken. It is understood and agreed to by all parties.

Once this happens, the rules of the teacher's union are forgotten. The starting date of the contract is now, and the teacher starts reading, planning, discussing, and learning. Supervisors hold formal and informal meetings with the staff, and plans are made to get things off the ground.

It is clear from the above that we depart from those who see a school that develops curriculum and determines pedagogical theory through committees or through consensus. We disagree with the view that says a school should represent all theoretical positions. Intellectual cowards want to have five viewpoints on discipline represented in a school, six theories of pedagogy, and four conceptions of the curriculum. Then, when a child fails to learn to behave or think, the other guy's theory can be blamed for the failure. We're all for setting up schools where each school thoroughly represents a different educational view and for giving those who run each school all they may require to implement that particular view. We may then find out which views are valid and which are based on old wives' tales.

Leadership, in our view, is not following the decisions of a committee. Leadership is marshaling forces to implement a theoretical schema. Theoretical schemas are thought out by scholars whose interest is in developing such theories. They are not constructed by tired teachers who have little interest in them in the first place and no training in their construction in the second place. Assign six teachers to a curriculum committee and in the first ten minutes someone will ask, "What does he want us to do?" and in the second ten minutes someone else will ask, "Why not write a number of other schools and see what they are doing?" Often the school to which the committee writes will have written to the first school at some time in the past and put some of its program into their own. Few teachers on a curriculum committee will ask, "What principle or law do we know that might lead us to believe this is a sound idea?"

Leadership, we have suggested, is in large part intellectual. It calls for reflection on a wide range of theoretical problems. The leader must solve these problems with the assistance of his supervisors and others concerned with theoretical matters. The teacher's main consideration must be his teaching and how it is affecting children. That is what he was hired to be — a teacher — not a curriculum man or an expert on instructional theory.

Once the supervisors and faculty have been hired and are ready to move to begin implementing the program, the leader should go before the PTA. Every effort should be made to ensure a large turnout for the meeting. The leadership in the PTA should be informed in advance what the program will include and the plans the staff has for the school. A straightforward presentation should be made, with a full rationale being made for the program. Many of the points developed in the first chapter of this book should be presented. While technical terms should be avoided, so should oversimplifications. A time schedule should be presented, and the need for paraprofessionals and teachers' aides should be indicated with a brief explanation of the qualifications needed for each role. It should be honestly pointed out that funds are lacking to do the job in grand style, that many problems must be faced, and that to make the program fully operative volunteers will be needed to supervise snack time and lunch periods. It should also be made clear that the staff is sincerely dedicated to the proposition that each child shall learn to read, write, and handle mathematics, as well as a number of other things, but that the staff cannot do it alone. The community must help. It should be made clear that success and/or innovation will lead to criticism and opposi-

154

tion, and again the local constituency of the school must help. It should be clear that the staff has taken on the responsibility of educating the young of that neighborhood and that, while it recognizes it is obligated to keep the community informed of what is happening to the young in school, and while it may even grant that the ultimate decision to retain or dismiss that staff rests with the community, the community must leave the staff free to exercise its professional judgments in order to demonstrate its competence or lack of competence. It should be understood that what is to be attempted is not the only means nor the only end that is educationally defensible. These are, however, the means and ends that this staff, at this point in its history, chooses to support and implement.

The presentation can, in our judgment, be made in 1½ hours. Another half hour can be given to answering questions. The PTA officers will then need to set up a means through which the parents can make a judgment to support or not to support the program. Other meetings, smaller in scope, may be needed to give additional answers to the community. Whatever the community requires in the way of information needed for judging the merits of the proposal should be given.

A meeting of the type we have just proposed can be significant to a school as it can signal the coming of a new period in school-community relations. The meeting must, at a minimum, accomplish two things. One, it must be the means, if not directly, then through hearsay, of bringing a sufficient number of people to the position that they will allow the staff to try to implement its program. Two, it must capture the interest of a small, potentially talented group who will function as paraprofessionals, teachers' aides, and volunteers and who will pursue their new endeavors with enthusiasm. The first, then, buys time. The second helps give you the means to implement your program. What more can one ask of a PTA?

TRAINING THE PARAPROFESSIONALS

The principal or leader should get to his PTA in the spring of the year and gain their support. He must then begin the process of hiring the paraprofessionals. Our experience, like everyone else's, is limited in this area. It would make sense to hire bright people. High school diplomas don't impress us as much as do native intelligence and desire. People with a sincere commitment to education would also seem to us important. We do not see dropping out of school and a commitment to education as mutually exclusive. People have been known to drop out of school in order to get an education. We are less sure of the following criteria, but perhaps adults in their late twenties or their thirties are the best bet. It may well be, though, that girls or boys in their late teens would do well. To us, they represent a bigger gamble, but if successful, this might prove to be the wiser move. We're not sure, and we can construct arguments both ways, but not with much conviction.

We would train more paraprofessionals than we needed and select the best to be employed on a regular basis. It would, of course, be explained to the candidates that more are being trained than are needed, that it is expected that some will find they are not interested, and that others may find they lack the talent necessary. Consequently, more must start in training than are needed, as we must be sure that we have enough paraprofessionals in September to carry out the program. Those not selected may have positions as teachers' aides and would be trained to fill any vacancies that might occur.

If the school ends up with ten paraprofessionals trained in mathematics when the program requires only four in the first grade and two in the second grade, the four extra ones could be used in the second-grade tutorial program for the first year, rather than using the four first-grade paraprofessionals. This would shorten the working day, increase the time available for training throughout the first year, and ensure a ready supply of experienced paraprofessionals to take the place of dropouts the second year, thereby eliminating the need for a summer training program the second year to train replacements.

There are five programs in which the paraprofessionals will function: the preschool program, the perception program in the kindergarten, the first-grade reading program, the first-grade mathematics program, and the tutorial and small-group programs in the second grade. Everyone working in these programs will need training in behavior-modification techniques. They will need to understand that they will have to make some decisions while working with children. The decisions they will need to make, they will be trained to make, so that they will not be left out in the cold. They will not have to decide what to teach, when to teach a particular thing, or how to teach. These questions will be handled by the supervisors in consultation with the teachers. The paraprofessionals will be supervised daily and will receive instruction, other information, and assistance each day, at which time they can also raise questions that are puzzling them. They may rest assured, however, that when they are working with the children, they are in charge, and they will not be interrupted or overridden in any manner. They may be taken to task later, but their position in front of the children will be maintained.

Let us now look at how the paraprofessional would be trained for the various programs. We use the reading program as an example. Naturally, variations in training would occur relative to the content to be taught by the particular group of paraprofessionals.

The most effective training, in our judgment, would be scheduled as follows: a two-week session, a two-week break, and then a one-week session. The first week should aim at familiarizing the paraprofessionals with the materials. Demonstration teaching by a teacher or supervisor familiar with the Words in Color program should be given. Visual and oral dictation should be given, with the paraprofessionals playing the role of students and the supervisor or teacher who is doing the demonstration teaching using the same techniques that are to be used with the children. The Words in Color worksheets should be worked through, and plenty of time should be given to working out transformations. Each paraprofessional should keep the results of this work in a notebook for future reference when working with the children in the fall.

The second week should be devoted to practice teaching, with supervisors and paraprofessionals playing student roles, while one paraprofessional acts as teacher. Teaching should be analyzed for behavior-modification strategies, strategies of data presentation, and other principles of teaching. Different principles of teaching should be concentrated on each day. During these two weeks, intensive study should be made of the signs presented in the first six or seven charts, with lists of words being developed that exist in the language and that are made up of the signs used on these charts, but which do not appear on the charts. Words that may be unfamiliar to the paraprofessional should be looked up in a dictionary and discussed. The last day of the second week should be given over to conferences between supervisors and trainees to discuss individual strengths and weaknesses. At this conference, a program of independent study to be followed by the trainee during the following two weeks should be laid out.

Upon returning to the school after the two-week study period, the last week should be devoted to a careful examination of what will happen in the first two weeks of the fall term. At this time, the staff and trainees should deal with such matters as the order of presenting material, the strategies to be used, the problems the children will face, the responses the children can be expected to give, happenings that should be considered significant, errors in teaching against which the trainees must guard, what help can be expected and at what times, etc. This discussion should be as detailed as possible and should anticipate as many contingencies as possible. Matters not directly related to teaching should also be covered, such as what to do in case of fire, a child becoming ill, a child wishing to go to the bathroom; availability of office space, if any; where to hang up one's coat; whom to call if sick. All of these things will help to put the trainee at ease and make him feel a part of the school. The last day ought to end with a congratulatory coffee hour being given by the supervisors for the new paraprofessionals.

The teachers' aides, we suggested earlier, could come from the ranks of the paraprofessionals or they might be employed directly as teachers' aides. We see the role of the teachers' aide as involving the following: producing and running off dittos, getting materials for the centers, assisting on trips, handling audio-visual equipment, handling routine reports, escorting children to lunch, getting out materials needed by the teachers and paraprofessionals, and generally assisting the staff with non-teaching matters. They may assist a child to construct something he needs in his work in the center, or they may accompany a child off the schoolground on a short errand relating to his work. The teachers' aide is, in short, the person who by being there enables the teaching staff to spend most of its time teaching children, rather than in preparing to teach children.

AVOIDING PROBLEMS OF IMPLEMENTATION

We now turn our attention to the beginning of the school year. Rather than discussing how to solve problems, we shall discuss how to avoid problems. Many of the problems to be avoided are of the kind we once faced with thirty-five college seniors in a remedial reading and mathematics program in a large urban school. From this experience, it is hoped we have learned something of value.

The first problem is that of teaching stations. The first-grade program, as it is set up here, calls for ten teaching stations each half hour for most of the morning. We start with four classrooms, and half of the youngsters are in two of these classrooms for language or independent study at any given time. This leaves two classrooms, and we have forty-eight children to be separated into eight groups, with six children in each group. Our experience indicates that two groups is the maximum that can work in a regular classroom. If this is done—and we recommend one reading group and one mathematics group in each classroom—then four of the eight groups are housed in the two remaining classrooms. The other four can be housed in the cafeteria, the remedial reading room if the school has one, the nurse's waiting room, storerooms, the end of a hall, the principal's office (he ought to be moving about the building), the auditorium, and any other available space. We have used all of these sites. The essential thing is to have a reasonably quiet place, a table, six chairs, a blackboard, and a place to put up the charts for reading.

The second way to avoid problems is by providing constant and close supervision. Every paraprofessional must be observed every day during the first two weeks. If one supervisor is responsible for supervising the eight first-grade paraprofessionals, he must watch each one for fifteen minutes each day. The coffee break should be used to make quiet suggestions, and the period from 11:05 A.M. until 12 noon should be used to give explicit descriptions of sound strategies that were employed and to explain why they were sound. When poor strategies are used, these should be explicitly described (by explicit we mean a verbal description of facial expressions, movements, exact dialogue, etc.), and the consequences of the poor strategy must be indicated. If only one paraprofessional is making a particular error, the discussion ought to be private. If several are making the same error, the problem should be dealt with in front of the whole group, though there is no necessity, of course, for naming names. Once a poor strategy has been identified and it is understood why it is a poor strategy, the supervisor must describe the strategy that should have been used. It goes without saying that the supervisor must be warm and supportive in what will be a trying experience for the paraprofessional.

158

The leader, other supervisors, and teachers should also make an effort to be supportive. It is particularly important that the leader do this. In the program we ran with the college students, the principal of the school wandered about the building, with members of the PTA and teachers on his staff, observing. Each day he was in the halls as the college girls left, asking if he could help in any way, reporting favorable comments from parents, making small talk, and in every way letting the girls know that he knew the problems they were facing, the conscientious efforts they were putting forth, their successes, and their failures. The girls appreciated his concern and support, and we suspect that more than one who had doubts as to whether she would make a good teacher got through a difficult program because Herman Bogden took the time to care. Mr. Bogden would say that all this was part of his job and no thanks are necessary. We agree. The point is that it is part of the leader's job to know what problems his staff is facing each day and to support his people so they can face those problems.

By the end of the third week, the supervisors should have identified the major strengths and weaknesses of each of the paraprofessionals. Individual programs should be set up to help the paraprofessionals overcome their major weaknesses.

The third way to avoid problems is for the staff to know at any given moment what is happening to each child. Much of what the supervisor does has to do with the performance of the staff under his direction. All that he does with these people must be related to the children and their progress. Through the questions he asks and the suggestions he makes, the supervisor should make it clear that the staff must be able at any given moment to state what any given child has learned in the past week and what problems the child is currently working to solve. Questions of the type, "How did your lesson go today?" are not as effective as, "What did José succeed in accomplishing today?" or, "Why do you think Ellie isn't getting the notion of addition?" The principal should ask this type of question of his staff as well as of the supervisors. The focus must be on what the children are accomplishing or not accomplishing. Successful teaching is related to children's learning, and it is only by looking at the children that you can determine the quality of the teaching.

The paraprofessionals are liable to be so concerned with their own performance that they won't see the children in front of their eyes. Their conversation will center on what they, themselves, are doing. The supervisor must bring them to realize that the important thing is what the children do.

The only other recommendation we can make is to have a sense of humor and some patience. A staff that can't laugh at itself is going to be a very poor staff.

Christmas vacation should give the staff a breather and time to reflect. The leader and supervisors will then need to consider reporting to the PTA. The report should include a brief review of what is being attempted, some description of the programs, some hard data on student performance, and other evidence that is available regarding the program's successes and failures. The parents then should be given a presentation relating to the setting up of the uncommon learning centers, the difficulties to be faced, and the assistance needed.

Another way of approaching the problem of keeping the parents informed of progress is to have the PTA set up an observer team in September, with appropriate guidelines to regulate their behavior, and have them take the responsibility for reporting to the parents. They will undoubtedly ask for assistance in making the presentation, and the leader should see that cooperation is given.

In either case, honesty should prevail. The schools are so bad that even the early stages of program development will look good by comparison. Furthermore, if the initial development of the program looks perfect, no one will feel obliged to help with the problems still to be faced.

PLANNING THE UNCOMMON LEARNING CENTERS

If one follows the timetable we have been following in this book, about the third week in October, when the school has settled into a routine, the paraprofessionals have gained some confidence, and the staff has developed some knowledge of each child and strategies for assisting each child to learn, the leader, supervisors, and teachers should bring together their thoughts on the uncommon learning centers. The leader should be prepared with a preliminary description of the physical plant that is available. Supervisors should have discussed with the paraprofessionals any ideas they might have for centers. Teachers should be clear as to what centers they wish to develop and be prepared to spell out these ideas in some detail. The spelling out should suggest procedures for others to follow in setting up centers.

When the meeting has ended, there should be a list of uncommon learning centers that you plan definitely to start, a list of centers you think you can start, and a list of centers you would like to have but see no way that they can be established. There should also have been a tentative discussion of the way in which the centers will be presented to the children, as well as discussion of the roles the children and adults will play in the centers. A small committee should be set up to coordinate activities, and assignments should be agreed upon relating to contacting people who might run centers, provide space or material, or assist in any other way. The chief function of the committee is to anticipate problems, suggest solutions, and prepare guidelines relating to the establishing and running of the centers. The committee should probably have no more than two members, as rarely do more than two members of any committee do any significant work.

Two weeks after this meeting, the leader needs to gather before him all the data he has relating to who will run what centers, what is needed for the

160

centers, how many centers there will be, and what loose ends need to be picked up. He then needs to make some judgments and discuss solutions with his committee. It may be that outside talent is needed. If so, informal contacts with the PTA might suggest persons who could run centers, or a university contact may yield talent that could be of use. The usual strategy is to appeal to undergraduate bodies. Our own suggestion is to appeal to colleges that run teacher-training programs for graduate students with liberal arts degrees. In these programs you can find mature women whose own children are in school and who are thus free to work in the early afternoon. Furthermore, these women usually have their classes at night, leaving them free for daytime activities. Because their classes are at night, they get little, if any, opportunity to work with children of the age they are being trained to teach. They have another virtue in that many of them have returned to the university because they wanted something more stimulating to do in life than keeping house. They believe they have talents that have atrophied. The uncommon learning centers will stimulate these women and give them a chance to develop their talents.

The sequence of events the leader must follow in setting up the centers is as follows:
1. Formulate a description of each center and the personnel to staff that center.
2. Have it clearly understood how, when, and under what rules the centers are to operate. Make clear the function of the centers.
3. Find a place to hold the centers.
4. Get whatever equipment and materials are necessary for the centers. Use the PTA.
5. Explain to the PTA the purpose of the centers, how they will be operated, and why they will be operated in this way.[2]
6. Educate the children as to the opportunities offered by the centers and the rules that govern participation in the centers.

SUPERVISION OF THE CENTERS

If the centers are to be successful, the leader and supervisors must constantly observe what is happening in the centers and assist those working in the centers to succeed. Problems will inevitably crop up. An outsider will be convinced he knows more about handling children than any teacher knows. Someone will run a popularity contest rather than an educationally sound enterprise. People will come up with wild ideas that are not workable but to which they are strongly attached, convinced that they are cure-alls for the problems of all the children. A paraprofessional with five months of teaching reading to small groups will conclude that the centers are not real education

[2] The term "PTA" is for our purposes synonymous with the term "community." Avenues of communication other than the PTA must be developed and used.

and will goof off and drink coffee all afternoon, or worse, turn the center into a reading clinic. Some centers will be popular with the children, while others of equal merit will not be. Some parents will push their children to go to centers of the parents' liking, not the child's. If some staff members feel the centers are a poor idea, one or two of them will work to prove they are right. Others who believe the program is a great idea will oversell it and misunderstand it. Conscientious, competent people will get so involved in doing something of value for the children that they will overlook an important institutional requirement. We once knew a teacher who planned a worthwhile trip with a fifth-grade class but forgot to notify the office of the exact date for his trip. The principal almost had apoplexy when he noted the empty classroom and couldn't locate twenty-four children and one teacher. All turned out well when they returned late in the afternoon, but the consequences could have been somewhat less than happy.

All the problems enumerated above cannot be completely avoided, nor can they always be fully solved. One can, however, do a number of things to avoid some of them and to mitigate the impact of others.

First, the leader and the supervisors must be in complete agreement as to what they are trying to do and how they are trying to do it, and they must have a clear understanding of their individual responsibilities. This may mean, among other things, dividing up responsibility for the several centers.

Second, careful screening when hiring is a must. The time to avoid mistakes is when you don't hire them. The innovator must have some gambling blood in his veins; but before hiring, there should be clear evidence that the person to be hired will be able to do the task at hand.

Third, while the centers are operating, the supervisors ought to be on the move, observing the centers, making notes, talking to children, watching teachers, seeing what materials are lacking, and noting traffic jams, poor procedures, pupil-teacher problems, etc.

Fourth, informal and formal meetings with individuals and groups should be held, at which time suggestions are made to staff, ideas are received from and explored with staff, complaints are heard, moral support is given, problems are faced, and successes are noted.

Fifth, careful records must be kept as to what centers are being attended by each child. The classroom teacher should be alerted to the kinds of learning experiences her children are getting during the time they are at the centers.

The key to the success of the centers lies in the ability of the supervisors to convey the impression that they fully support the program, that they know what is going on, that they can help to solve problems, that they believe in the children and the staff, that the program will succeed, that hysteria isn't needed, and that those who won't or cannot succeed will be removed. Regarding this last point, we should like to counter the notion that the dismissal of someone is necessarily bad for staff morale. Our own view is that the firing of incompetents is a tremendous morale booster for those who are competent. If the goals are high, the criteria for continuance tough, and the mortality rate is high enough, then two things result: anxiety, of course, but also pride and desire in those who survive. There is little satisfaction in making a team that judges everyone's work as satisfactory.

EVALUATING THE CENTERS

The other thing the supervisors must do jointly with the staff is to evaluate the centers. Success will, of course, be determined by student growth. The criteria for evaluation should be developed from the outset with the staff. The accomplishments of all centers will not yield to quantitative analysis, and you undoubtedly won't have the staff to work out the means of quantifying the results of some that might. You will then have two kinds of data. We shall call them hard data and soft data. Hard data would be those that can be measured and quantified by a test of ability. An achievement-test score would be one example. Another example would be a record that shows that Billy Jackson spent forty minutes of each hour goofing off during the first two weeks but wasted no time at all during the second two weeks. An example of soft data would be, perhaps, a mother's report that a child who formerly disliked school, since going to the arts and crafts center, jumps out of bed, eats, and rushes off to school.

Whether the distinction between soft and hard data is a valid one, we are not sure. The problem, in any event, is how one interprets the data one has and what data one puts stock in. The difficulty with quantifying is that many important things are not easily quantified. It is not easy to measure respect for property, pride, language that reveals a growing positive self-concept, love of learning, and growing reasoning abilities. We feel, however, that these factors are at least as important as a reading score that can be quantified. The key in evaluation is change — change that can be viewed as growth. Examples would be the use of a new word; the application of some new knowledge; a new awareness; a new behavior; increased verbalism; verbalism that increasingly gives an accurate description of reality; increased enthusiasm for learning and living; a different kind of question being asked; a new logic being used; an awareness of a strategy that is employed; a reduction in tattling, lateness, punching, shouting, inattentiveness, and other self-defeating forms of behavior; increased determination in the face of a difficult problem; etc. The sum total of all the things a child does, plus all the new things all the other children do, will reveal the general changes that take place in a school.

The first two weeks the centers are in operation will reveal much random activity on the part of the children. At times, chaos will seem to be the order of the day, but as each child finds purpose in some activity, order will result, and the change will be easily discerned. Law and order flow as a natural consequence of children finding purpose in an activity. Law and order must be imposed in prison because the inmates can see no purpose in what they do. Learning is also a consequence of children finding purpose in what they are doing. And the goal of a school is learning, not law and order. Law and order are by-products of children who are busy learning, not the other way around. A school that is spending its time imposing law and order has things backwards.

CONDUCTING SCHOLARSHIP WEEK

We need now to make a few remarks about the administering of scholarship week. The purposes of scholarship week are several:

1. The primary purpose is to honor scholarship. A community conveys to its youth what it honors. If it honors rioting in the streets, it will have children who will riot in the streets. If it honors athletics, it will get athletes. If it honors scholarship, it will get scholars.
2. In the day-to-day process of learning, a child often fails to fully appreciate how much progress he has made. A week in which his work is on display gives him time to reflect on how much progress he has made.
3. A school must have the courage to say, "This is the result of our efforts. We cannot show you all we have accomplished, but we can show you enough so that you can judge our competence and come to appreciate what we are striving to accomplish."
4. Scholarship week gives the children a chance to cooperate in a large effort, to function as part of a social institution, and to identify with that institution.
5. Because scholarship week is a large effort that goes beyond the school in a different manner, opportunities for a number of learning experiences are presented.

PLANNING THE SECOND YEAR

What specific problems one will face the second year are hard to guess from this vantage point. How well one can plan will obviously depend on how much data one has on the first year's experience and how well one can interpret the data. If one still clearly sees one's goals and can see where one has failed and where one has succeeded and can then assess how to overcome the failures while maintaining the successes, the job is done. But that is to say the obvious. In reality, the task is the same as when one started. One is just at a different point in the journey with different assets and different debits. Hopefully, one is also a little wiser.

What is clear is that in the course of the first year the leader should have devoted considerable attention, particularly in the last four months, to gathering any and all data and judgments that might prove relevant. Clearly, more training of staff for the second-year programs will be necessary. Clearly, the time for taking it easy has not come.

SELECTED BIBLIOGRAPHY

BEHAVIOR MODIFICATION

Bandura, A.: "Behavioral Psychotherapy," *Scientific American*, 216:78-86, March, 1967.

_____ and R. H. Walters: *Social Learning and Personality Development*, New York, Holt, Rinehart and Winston, Inc., 1963.

Buehler, R. E., G. R. Patterson, and J. M. Furniss: "The Reinforcement of Behavior in Institutional Settings," *Behavior Research and Therapy*, 4:147–167, 1966.

Eysenck, H. J.: *Experiments in Behavior Therapy*, New York, Pergamon Press, Inc., 1964.

Ferster, C. B., and Jeanne Simons: "Behavior Therapy with Children," *Psychological Record*, 16:65–71, 1965.

Hotchkiss, James: "The Modification of Maladaptive Behavior of a Class of Educationally Handicapped Children by Operant Conditioning Techniques," paper presented at the American Educational Research Association, Los Angeles, February, 1969.

Spaulding, Robert L.: *Classroom Behavior Analysis and Treatment Using the Coping Analysis Schedule for Educational Settings (CASES) and the Spaulding Teacher Activity Rating Schedule (STARS)*, Durham, N.C., Education Improvement Program, Duke University, 1968.

Ullman, L. P., and L. Krasner: *Case Studies in Behavior Modification*, New York, Holt Rinehart and Winston, Inc., 1965.

CONCEPT FORMATION AND DISCOVERY METHODS

Almy, Millie, et al.: *Young Children's Thinking*, New York, Bureau of Publications, Teachers College, 1966.

Ausubel, David P.: "Learning by Discovery: Rationale and Mystique," *National Association of Secondary School Principals Bulletin*, 45:18–58, December, 1961.

Bruner, Jerome S., Jacqueline J. Goodnow, and George A. Austin: *A Study of Thinking*, New York, John Wiley and Sons, Inc., 1956.

_____, Rose R. Olver and Patricia M. Greenfield: *Studies in Cognitive Growth*, New York, John Wiley and Sons, Inc., 1966.

Flavell, John H.: *The Developmental Psychology of Jean Piaget*, Princeton, N.J., D. Van Nostrand Co., Inc., 1963.

Hendrix, Gertrude: "Prerequisite to Meaning," *The Mathematics Teacher*, 43:334–339, 1950.

Inhelder, Barbel, and Jean Piaget: *The Early Growth of Logic in the Child*, New York, Harper and Row, 1964.

Postman, Neil, Harold Morine, and Greta Morine: "The Inductive Lesson," in *Discovering Your Language*, teachers' ed., New York, Holt, Rinehart and Winston, 1963, pp. 6–16 of the Teacher's Guide.

Shulman, Lee S., and Evan R. Keisler: *Learning by Discovery: A Critical Appraisal*, Chicago, Rand, McNally and Company, 1966.

Taba, Hilda: "Learning by Discovery: Psychological and Educational Rationale," *Elementary School Journal*, 63:308–316, March, 1963.

PERCEPTION TRAINING

Delacato, Carl H.: *Diagnosis and Treatment of Speech and Reading Problems*, Springfield, Ill., Charles C. Thomas, Publisher, 1963.

Frostig, Marianne, and David Horne: *The Frostig Program for Development of Visual Perception: Teachers' Guide*, Chicago, Follett Publishing Co., 1964.

Getman, Gerald N., and Elmer R. Kane: *The Physiology of Readiness*, Minneapolis, Minn., Programs to Accelerate School Success, Inc., 1964.

Johnson, Orville G.: *Education for the Slow Learner*, New York, The Ronald Press Co., 1960.

Kephart, Newell C.: *The Slow Learner in the Classroom*, Columbus, Ohio, Charles E. Merrill Books, Inc., 1960.

Money, John: *Reading Disability*, Baltimore Md., Johns Hopkins Press, 1963.

Mosston, Muska: *Developmental Movement*, Columbus, Ohio, Charles E. Merrill Books, Inc., 1955.

Rambush, Nancy: *Learning How to Learn*, Baltimore Md., Helicon Press, 1962.

Roach, Eugene G., and Newell C. Kephart: *The Purdue Perceptual-Motor Survey*, Columbus, Ohio, Charles E. Merrill Books, Inc., 1966.

Sutphin, Florence E.: *A Perceptual Testing and Training Handbook for First Grade Teachers*, Winter Haven, Fla., Winter Haven Lions Research Foundation, Inc., 1964.

INSTRUCTIONAL GUIDES

Gattegno, C.: *For the Teaching of Elementary Mathematics*, Vols. I, II, and III, New York, Cuisenaire Company of America, Inc., 1964.

_____: *Mathematics with Numbers in Color*, Books I and II, New York, Cuisenaire Company of America, Inc., 1959.

_____: *Teaching Reading with Words in Color*, New York, Educational Solutions, Inc., 1968.

Gilbert, Edna: *A Way with Words*, New York, Educational Solutions, Inc., 1968.

Murphy, Sister Mary Leonore: *Douglas Can Read*, New York, Educational Solutions, Inc., 1968.

_____: *Barnaby*, available from Educational Solutions, Inc., 1968.

_____: *Creative Writing*, available from Educational Solutions, Inc., 1966.

Veatch, Jeanette: *Individualizing Your Reading Program*, New York, G. P. Putnam's Sons, 1959.

TESTS

Bender, Lauretta: *Bender Visual-Motor Gestalt Test for Children*, Western Psychological Services, Los Angeles, 1964.

Benton, A. L.: *Benton Visual Retention Test*, 3d ed., The Psychological Corporation, New York, 1963.

Dunn, L. M.: *Peabody Picture Vocabulary Test*, American Guidance Service, Minneapolis, 1959.

Kirk, Samuel A., Winifred Kirk, and J. J. McCarthy: *Illinois Test of Psycholinguistic Abilities*, University of Illinois Press, Urbana, 1968.

Lazarus, Phoebe W.: *Visuo-Motor Designs* (Lazarus Copy Forms), Lazarus Visuo-Motor Diagnostic Sequence, Phoebe W. Lazarus, 167 Kings Point Road, Great Neck, New York.

White, Mary Alice., and Marian Phillips: *White-Phillips Visual Motor Test;* "The Psycho-Physiological Predictors of School Performance Using Group Scoring Techniques." A report given at American Orthopsychiatric Association, Chicago, Ill., 1964. (Manual available from Dr. White, School Psychology Dept., Teachers College, Columbia University.)

Wepman, Joseph: *Auditory Discrimination Test*, Language Research Associates, Chicago, 1958.

INDEX

169